Based on a Tr...

Joey Cassata
&
Christopher Lynn

Wrestling with joeylicious

Joey Cassata
Christopher Lynn

Book 1

Published by Satta Entertainment
Written by Joey Cassata & Christopher Lynn
Book design by Joey Cassata
Cover design by Joey Cassata & Carlos Espada
Front and Back Cover photo by Dominic Peluso
Edited by Vanessa Richie, Joey Cassata & Christopher Lynn
Joeylicious Character Created by Joey Cassata

© Copyright 2020 Satta Entertainment and Lynstrumental Entertainment. All rights reserved.

All rights reserved. No part of this book may be reproduced in any form or by any electronic or mechanical means, including information storage or retrieval systems, without the written consent of copyright owner, except in the case of brief quotations embodied in articles and reviews.

What the Wrestling World is saying about Wrestling With Joeylicious...

"Joeylicious is exactly what the wrestling world needs right now. It's funny, creative and features some of the best names in history."

- Mick Foley

"I really like this (Joeylicious) idea!"

- Hulk Hogan

"Like me, Joey Cassata loves music, wrestling and comedy. Plus, he's a great guy with an 'always be hustling' attitude. Now if he would only do something about that nose.... Anyhoo, READ THIS BOOK!"

-Chris Jericho

"It would be an honor to work with the Joeylicious."

-The Iron Sheik

"I think Joey is onto something really good. I really like this idea."

-Tito Santana

"I want to be in this baby!"

- "The Mouth of the South" Jimmy Hart

Chapters

1. The Italian Dream..1
2. B.R.A.W.L..8
3. The Hulkster & Highlights.............................17
4. Fr. Randazzo & Tighty Whities.....................25
5. Obstacle Course of Doom..............................37
6. A Tiny Slam from Glory.................................42
7. The True Cost of Priceless.............................50
8. 10 or 15% of Anne-Marie...............................57
9. Golden God & Asian Goddesses...................65
10. The Fifth Horseman.......................................71
11. Rapid Firing Sex Machine..........................,..75
12. Three's a Confessional Crowd....................80
13. Bingo & B.R.A.W.L 85
14. The Four Faces of Foley...............................92
15. The Intervention...101
16. Small Helmet, Smaller Office....................106
17. Milk Shakes, Payoffs & Young Guns.................114
18. Gehrig's Ghost...122

19. Race War! 128

20. The Flying Irishman...135

21. Guilt by Association..144

22. "Life is a Ring"..149

23. With a Little Help to His Friends..............................156

24. Too Sweat to be Sour..162

25. 50 Cents?! What?! 170

26. No Time to Pack! 177

27. Enter Sandman..185

28. The Vegan Who Wasn't There..................................191

29. 100 Miles to Hulkster Heaven..................................197

30. Samurai Dwayne..204

31. Imposter?! 210

Epilogue..218

Chapter 1
The Italian Dream

As sound blared from the static ridden, colored TV inside a modest, two bedroom Brooklyn apartment, a pair of ten-year-old boys mimicked the noise levels from home. Looking at them, it was hard to imagine that they were the same age. Joey Cassata, with his olive skin and jet black hair, making his Italian heritage easily detectable, was already the size of a high school football player. His best friend, Robert Scally, on the other hand, was tiny even for a fourth grader. The blonde crew cut made the lad of Irish heritage look more menacing than his 4'3 stature suggested, but his scrawny, pale meat hooks couldn't lift a beanbag an inch off the floor if duty called.

Her arms folded across her chest, Joey's mom, Mrs. Cassata, was resigned to the antics of her son and his crony. Planted between the two boys, bouncing back and forth like a pinball, the thirty-five-year-old hoped to minimize the damage, but it was obvious from her expression that she knew it was a lost cause. With the 1984 WWF title match playing out on screen live from Madison Square Garden via the MSG Network, with their favorite wrestler, Hulk Hogan, facing off against one of the most notorious heels in wrestling, The Iron Sheik, there was little hope that she would achieve much more than a few bruises from the overexcited youngsters.

Joey barely kept his butt on the couch as his eyes were glued to the events unfolding on TV. His hair, worn long and flowing over his broad shoulders, was clearly styled to look like his blonde hero Hulk Hogan. Already 5'6 and 150 pounds, it was easy to imagine him one day being able to step into the ring, though at the moment, Mrs. Cassata would have been happy for him to just act as mature as he looked. All he needed was a few more years of growing at his current pace, and he would be more than big enough to join the world that so fascinated him. Despite it being clear that Scally would never be large enough to follow his friend's athletic path, the young boy was just as pumped about the match before them.

"C'mon, Hulkster," Joey yelled at the TV. His mother leaned away from him, but quickly righted herself as equally enthusiastic chatter spewed from her son's playmate.

"The Sheik can't win this, can he?" Scally's words had started out with confidence, but uncertainty at what was unfolding on the screen made him queasy.

Joey had no such crisis of faith. "Not a chance, Scal! Get with it! The Hulkster could beat this sneaky Uranium with one arm if he had to!"

"Iranian," Mrs. Cassata corrected. It was no wonder her son was getting C's in both Science and Geography.

Ignoring the lesson in both subjects, Scally had more pressing issues. "He gets Hogan in that 'camel clutch,' it's over. No one ever escapes that." It was something both boys had whispered about as being the only possible way the Iron Sheik could win, so it was a legitimate concern.

Almost as if the Iron Sheik had heard that fear straight through the TV, he maneuvered around the Hulkster and wrapped his beefy arms around their heroes neck.

"No," Joey yelled as if he was personally locked in the struggle himself.

"I jinxed it," Scally declared, certain that this travesty

wouldn't have happened if he had simply kept his big mouth shut.

Reaching over his mother, Joey showed that he agreed with this assessment. Shoving his best friend with the accidental force of Lenny from Of Mice and Men, he knocked Scally clear off of the couch.

Mrs. Cassata glared like a laser at her bully of a son. "Joey, play nice," she shouted louder than the boys and TV combined.

"Impossible," her son responded, too caught up in the moment to care what he had done.

Scally scrambled back onto the couch, accepting his punishment, but unwilling to miss any more of the action. Both boys watched in rapt awe as their hero did the impossible. As the MSG crowd cheered, the great blonde giant broke free from the "camel clutch," and turned on his opponent.

"Yes," Joey yelled.

"Let's go, Hogan! Win this thing," Scally screamed.

Mrs. Cassata ignored the assault on her entire being, her own attention now focused on the televised event.

Once free of that impossible grip, the Hulkster grabbed the current WWF Champion and tossed him against the ropes. The Iron Sheik flailed wildly as he tried to regain his balance. Seeing his opportunity, Hogan moved in and delivered his own signature move, the "big boot," which was simply a kick to the face. Unable to withstand the blow, the Sheik went down. Hogan then made certain that his foreign foe remained canvas fodder by finishing him off with his equally famous "leg drop," which was simply a drop of the leg onto his opponent's neck. Hogan was not reinventing sliced bread here, but then again sliced bread never caused this much pain. As the Sheik moved groggily on the mat, the Hulkster pinned him.

As soon as the referee counted to three, the boys exploded

with the sound of the bell ringing on TV. They hooted and hollered as they leapt up and down on the couch, ultimately hugging over the preordained outcome. All Mrs. Cassata could manage was a worn smile as the boys seemed to forget that she was still in between them. After a minute of celebration, she finally broke the spell.

"Alright, you two. Take it easy." Her tone was more lighthearted than a warning, but it still left a hint that her mood could suddenly change for the worse.

The celebration on TV continued, but Joey seemed to have returned to the present, or at least returned to himself. A Zen-like quality came over him. "I have to win that belt someday."

Mrs. Cassata looked at her son as he stepped off the couch, her expression clearly softening. She knew, or at least prayed, that by the time Joey was an adult, such wild notions would be long gone.

Scally, on the other hand, had no such sage insight from which to draw his reaction. Joey's words struck a chord in him. "Of course! You'll be a beast! Look at you now at 10!"

Joey smiled. "I picked out a name already."

"Really? What is it?"

Joey's grin widened, but he wasn't about to spoil the surprise.

Scally grabbed the front of his shirt. "Tell me!" His voice was between pleading and threatening, but neither would work on his best friend. At least not yet.

* * * * *

Joey stood behind an old dirty curtain, rocking back and forth with anticipation as the ring announcer pulled the mic closer to his face. "Here to bring the violence for you all

WRESTLING WITH JOEYLICIOUS

tonight is the man of the hour, the tower of power, too sweet to be sour, the Italian dream – Joeylicious!"

The Saint Patrick's Gymnasium wasn't a particularly large place for Saturday night wrestling with a max seating capacity of 150 on the surrounding rickety bleachers, but the boos that immediately sounded at the end of the announcer's words echoed as if they were delivered from the Grand Canyon. The Irish grammar school was noisy all day, so this was just par for the course. What was different was the way the gym had been setup. Cheap banners welcomed the roughly 25 deadbeat fans to Brooklyn's Really Awesome Wrestling League, or B.R.A.W.L. And, although the max seating capacity was 150, this was considered a sell-out. Welcome to the lowest rung of the wrestling world.

Joeylicious stepped out into the gym with his arms in the air. As soon as he emerged, the crowd began throwing things at him. After more than 20 years of wrestling experience, Joeylicious was quite accustomed to this response as he climbed into the ring. The years hadn't been particularly kind to him. He had only grown another five inches since he was 10 years old, reaching 5'11 by the time he turned 20. Now in his 40s, his once rippling muscles weren't so rippling, and the genesis of a bulging gut was beginning to form. Still, he was in remarkably good spirits considering his current state. His outfit was a black singlet with red boas and a cape, making him look more like a WWF villain from the 1980s than a present day hero. His hair was still long, but he had added blonde highlights to his black locks, at least partly to hide the grey hairs he had started to notice.

"And his opponent-" the crowd immediately began to cheer over the announcer's words forcing him to pull the mic even closer, "bringing his extraordinary looks and luck with him all the way from Ireland – built like a rock and ready to sock, the undefeated Irish Assassin … Paddy Shamrock!"

The cheers grew deafening as a tall, muscular twenty-one-year-old stepped out and headed toward the ring. As he approached Joeylicious, there was clear contempt on his face. Paddy Shamrock offered his hand, but quickly pulled it back as Joeylicious reached out to shake it. Paddy ran his fingers through his hair and turned to the small crowd with a wide grin on his face.

One undersized fan of the Italian sacrificial lamb stood up on the back bleacher. Still Joey's best friend and now also his manager, Scally hadn't grown much either, peaking at only 5'5 and still very scrawny. The white, wife beater tank top he wore didn't do his small arms any favors, more highlighting his fragile bones than drawing attention to his puny muscles. Holding a Styrofoam cup of beer, Scally glared down at the crowd favorite. "Suck it, Shamrock!"

Beside him, a filthy looking man with a massive beer gut turned his attention. "Sit down, you drunk!"

Suddenly aware of the bleacher rival, Scally sensed a chance to unleash some of his own tension. "Hey, this is the visitors section!"

"There is no visitors section!" The man was clearly exasperated.

"I just claimed it," Scally shot back as if he was hoping for a fight.

But before anything could erupt between them, the bell rang, signaling the beginning of the fight everyone had paid for. Not willing to waste another second on Scally, the man rolled his eyes and faced the ring. "Loser," he muttered.

Scally, thankfully missing the cold dis, also turned his attention to the two "professional" combatants.

WRESTLING WITH JOEYLICIOUS

Unfortunately, it was very clear early on that Joeylicious didn't stand a chance. After being tossed around like a rag doll and being the recipient of several body slams, pile drivers, and clotheslines, it seemed as if the Italian Dream wouldn't even get in a single good shot. Or a bad shot. Or any shot. Climbing back up on his feet, though, Joeylicious took Paddy by surprise. With a burst of energy, he managed to get in a solid jab to his opponent's face, sending Paddy down to the canvas. The crowd let out a gasp, and Joeylicious played his sudden good fortune up. Holding his arms in the air, he strutted close to the ropes to get more of a reaction from the blood thirsty fans of the young Irishman, who, let's face it, wasn't really from Ireland.

From behind, Paddy caught Joeylicious off guard with an elbow to the back of his head. The Italian Dream's view of the audience quickly changed to a view of the asbestos ridden ceiling above him. Paddy came into view, and Joeylicious knew exactly what was coming next. Paddy was tall, but not that tall. Clearly, he had climbed onto the top rope. With a stunning splash, he crashed onto Joeylicious and pinned him until the ref counted to three.

The crowd burst into cheers for their fighter. Everyone except Scally, who was now itching for a fight of his own. "Foul! Disqualification!".

Beside Scally, Paddy's beer gutted fan took offense. "Are you gonna start that again?"

His temper unchecked, Scally chucked his now empty Styrofoam cup at the fan, smacking him square in the face. The fan immediately responded by attacking Scally. Just like his best friend, Scally didn't stand a chance. Visitors section or not.

Chapter 2
B.R.A.W.L.

After wiping his sweaty face with a towel, Joey wrapped it around his neck and moved over to the bench of St. Pat's locker room. Flopping down, he felt a bit defeated. Well, more than a bit. He just got his ass kicked. The other three wrestlers present largely ignored him as they had their own miseries to deal with.

When Lou Rossati entered, all heads turned his way. Was this the school janitor? No, this short, stubby, greasy man who would finish runner up to Danny Devito in a beauty contest if such a beauty contest existed actually ran the day to day operations of BRAWL. And he was "thrilled" to this fact.

Joey already had a beef. "Lou, does Shamrock have his own trailer or what? He never showers with us."

Lou shrugged. "Whatta you wanna wash his balls?"

It soon became clear that Joey wasn't the only one suspicious of his wannabe Irish rival. Una Granada, a once handsome Latino, now well passed his prime, was no fan either. "I hear he's being groomed for high school venues." His tone was more of an accusation than a question.

Joey shook his head despondently. "Lost to him three times already!"

Lou shrugged again. "You're Italian. It's a rivalry." It was obvious that he was evading what the men really wanted to know.

WRESTLING WITH JOEYLICIOUS

Joey pointed over to a tall, trim African-American who looked more like a basketball player than a wrestler. "What about Milk Shake? The Irish get along with the Blacks all of a sudden?"

Suddenly pulled into the conversation, Milk Shake didn't feel any better off. "He beat my ass four times."

"Ridiculous," Joey said, his eyes refocused on Lou.

Trying to blow off the concern, Lou gave them all a look of whatever-ness. Then he threw Joey a bone. "Quit whining. You win next week on your home turf."

This was news to Joey. "We're at S.T.A. next week?"

Knowing that was the perfect distraction, Lou grinned. "Happy now?"

"Yeah, baby," the grammar school alumni answered enthusiastically as he pumped his fist.

"You beat Tiny."

This was less welcome news. Joey turned to the massively overweight man who looked like a reformed skinhead who had spent too many years on the couch attacking ice cream bars instead of barbells. "What? No!" He looked back at Lou.

At nearly the same time, Tiny glanced up. "What'd I do?"

Joey vigorously shook his head. "How am I supposed to beat Tiny convincingly? I can't even lift him!"

"Shamrock slams me," Tiny shrugged, exposing a few tatoos in the process.

The Italian Dream waved a dismissive hand. "Tiny, I don't wanna hear it. I love you, but you're enormous."

Before anyone else could chime in, an unwelcome Scally strolled in with a huge grin on his lips and a large ice pack over his eye. "Heck of a job tonight, fellas. Heck of a job." His voice beamed with pride as he thought about the events of the evening.

WRESTLING WITH JOEYLICIOUS

There was a round of half-hearted hellos before most of the men returned to what they were doing before Lou had entered.

"How is it you always look more beat up than me?" Joey griped at his so-called manager.

Like Lou, Scally chose to avoid answering the question directly. His tactic was a bit more obvious though. "Any drink tickets left?"

"I gave you all mine already. Milk Shake's too."

Scally turned to the man with the Kevin Durant physic, albeit a foot shorter. "Yeah, thanks, Chocolate Milk Shake."

"It's Milk Shake," the African-American wrestler shot back.

"Well, you're black so I figured –"

This caused Milk Shake to break things down for the accidental bigot: "And you're white, but I just call you cracker! Not vanilla cracker – just plain cracker!"

"They don't have vanilla crackers. I'd have to be a cookie," Scally chuckled at how clever he felt.

As if it was the most natural thing in the world, Tiny moved away from his locker and strode toward the shower wearing only a small towel around his waist. This had the unfortunate effect of a beach whale covering his privates with a napkin.

Una Granada held up his hands. "Whoa, my man!" His wavy hair moved with his motions as did a bit of his own fat that had accumulated around his mid section.

Joey averted his eyes fearing what could happen next. "Tiny!"

"Damn," Milk Shake added to the protests.

"Didn't we get you that extra-large robe last month?" Una Grenada had to ask.

"It's in the wash. What? I can't take a shower?" Tiny's tone showed complete indifference to the ill feelings around him.

Ushering the big man along, Una Granada hoped that he

would just be out of sight before the towel decided to succumb to gravity. "All yours."

As Tiny strode out of view, Lou brought the focus back to himself. "Alright, let me pay you dummies and get outta here."

Milk Shake stepped forward with a glow. "That's what I'm talkin' about!"

As he handed out the cash, Lou announced: "By the way, everybody bring your 'A' game next week. We may have a special visitor."

A curious Una Grenada peered up from his earnings. "Who?"

"Just bring it, alright, Una Granada?"

Joey beamed down at his greenbacks. "Nice! $47.50!"

"Sweet," his best friend chimed in. Then he snatched the money out of Joey's hand. "Meet you at the bar!" With that, Scally exited in a flash.

Still not dressed to leave, all Joey could do was reach desperately for the air. "Damn it, Scally! Get back here!" Rethinking the matter, he quickly grabbed his stuff and ran out as well.

* * * * *

The pair arrived at the Cassata apartment well into the night, making far too much noise as they entered. It was the same apartment from Joey's childhood, and it hadn't changed much at all. Yes, Joey still lived with his mom. $47.50 only went so far, whether he kept it away from Scally or not. "Quiet," he whispered to his drunk friend.

Offended by the demand, Scally glared back. "What'd I say?"

"Joey, is that you?" the familiar voice of Mrs. Cassata

greeted the pair from another part of the apartment.

Joey hit his friend in the chest. "Yeah, Ma! Go back to sleep!"

Scally rubbed his chest, muttering about the abuse being dished out.

"Scally's with you?" The pair froze at the dreaded question that was more of a statement.

"It's Saturday," Joey finally responded indirectly, doing his best to avoid lying to his mother.

She was hardly appeased. "I'm going to eight o'clock mass in the morning! Keep it down!"

With that, Joey knew the jig was up. "We will!"

Scally stumbled into the wall.

"You alright?" his one and only client asked while steadying him.

"Man, I gotta stop drinkin'," Scally slurred back. "I'll grab some beers from the fridge," the little man added as he stumbled through the door.

Knowing that the lush would at least take great care when procuring alcohol, Joey simply shook his head at the mixed message.

* * * * *

Joey's bedroom hadn't changed much since he was 10; in the same way Joey hadn't changed period. It was a wrestling shrine! Posters and memorabilia of WWF, WWE, NWA, AWA and WCW legends were everywhere. Not surprisingly, all things Hulk Hogan were especially prominent. In a way, Joey was a relic trapped inside a room of other relics.

Sprawled out on the bed, Scally downed a beer while watching Joey pace. "Quit sulkin' already and drink up." His hand missed picking up a fresh beer on the first attempt, but managed to secure one on the second. Taking aim, he threw the cool beverage to his sober friend. Or at least he hoped it was to him. The sound of the bottle smashing against the wall proved otherwise.

Joey glared at the misfiring troublemaker.

"C'mon, Joe, ruined a perfectly good beer," Scally still accused.

"You're cleaning this up," Joey hissed back. If he had expected Scally to chuck a beer his way, he may have caught it. When did Scally ever part with a beer, anyway?

Scally shot up at his words. "That's it," he shouted far too loud. "First thing tomorrow we start gettin' you back in shape! Five o'clock sharp!"

Joey gave his so-called manager a withered look. "You'll be hungover at five AM."

"No, I'll still be drinking. Five PM," he clarified with pride.

Joey rolled his eyes. "Right. First thing." His best friend's antics weren't doing much to bolster his spirits, so he sat down heavily on the foot of his bed and just stared at the floor.

Seeing that his friend was particularly dejected, Scally went into true managerial mode. With great reluctance, he put his beers aside. "Do that new combination on me."

Joey looked up at the blonde imp. It was a nice gesture, but there was no chance he would try it on Scally. "It's devastating. You'll break something."

Scally hopped around like a one-legged boxer. "No, I won't."

"Okay, you'll separate something. Like when I messed up your shoulder at Chrissy Manns's Sweet 16."

Scally stopped moving. "I'm a man now!"

"You're a toothpick," Joey shot back.

~ 13 ~

WRESTLING WITH JOEYLICIOUS

Realizing there was only way to get his much larger friend to spring into action, Scally put Joey in a headlock. "C'mon, bring the violence!"

The hold had little to no effect on the wrestler. "Would you cut it out? I'm tired."

"I'll choke you out, punk ass!"

Finally without warning, Joey grabbed his tiny friend, flipped him over, and tossed him into the wall. Well, not into the wall exactly; more like through the wall for Scally was now embedded upside down inside the sheetrock. Scally looked up helplessly. He was good and stuck.

The bedroom door flew open. "Robert Scally, what did you do?" Mrs. Cassata stood in the doorway, her grey hair pinned up in rollers and her pink nightgown flowing with the breeze she created when she made her dramatic entrance. She looked more like an aging Valkyrie than Joey's mother.

"What did I do?" Scally protested from his unmovable position.

Something else caught Mrs. Cassata's attention. "And whatta surprise! Beers!" Her glare turned to her son. "You know I can't stand when he drinks in here!"

"I had like 10, 11 beers. So what?" Scally pleaded his case further.

Of course, this was the wrong thing to say to the already fuming sixty-five-year-old woman. "Get outta this apartment," she screamed.

"Ma, you said he could sleep over," Joey bemoaned, feeling betrayed.

"You wanna go, too?"

Joey knew it was useless arguing with his mother in her state, so he just yanked Scally out of the wall. This caused further pain to his friend, and an even larger whole in the wall. Mrs.

~ 14 ~

WRESTLING WITH JOEYLICIOUS

Cassata could only shake her head in disappointment, as her son tossed the drunken Scally over his shoulder and carried him away.

* * * * *

After making sure Scally got home safely, Joey stood in front of his friend's parents' house watching him fumble with the key to the front door. It was quite the ordeal. After dropping the key onto the porch a few times and trying to use it in the broken doorbell at least twice, the drunk managed to stagger through the threshold. Feeling that his job was finally done for the night, Joey turned and headed back home.

Once inside the house, Scally tripped over the shoe rack and hit the floor. Deciding that it wasn't worth the effort to stand, he crawled across the living room to the area near the window that was usually cool. Only the window was shut. Focusing on what was in front of him, he suddenly realized that he had to use the bathroom. Badly. In a haze, Scally thought he could see the toilet. Not entirely sure how he managed to reach the bathroom so quickly, he used the wall to haul himself off the floor. Staggering around, he undid his pants and took aim at the middle toilet. He currently saw at least three. Once he finished relieving himself, Scally let gravity run its course. He crashed to the floor, and drifted off to sleep.

The lush wasn't aware of the sound of descending footsteps, or even the short, dark figure that was suddenly looming over him.

"Christ," the figure muttered. Looking down at the spread eagle disgrace on the floor, the older man with blondish white hair shook his head in disgust. It was obvious by the look on his face that this was nothing new. In fact it was usually much worse. Or so he thought.

"Get up, dummy." Scally's father nudged his son with his foot. Apart from the slipper seeming to tickle the drunk, there was no real reaction. Taking a deep breath and wiping beads of sweat from his forehead, the poor man was clearly at a loss and uncomfortable. "100 degrees down here," he muttered, his attention now more on his own discomfort than the regular sight of his son passed out.

Leaning over his son, the older man turned on the fan. But instead of the relief he hoped to receive from cool air, Mr. Scally felt liquid coming off the fan. Perplexed, he stepped away from it. "What the-"

Quickly turning off the fan, Mr. Scally wiped the new wetness off his face and sniffed to see if he could detect what it was. He immediately scrunched up his face and held his hand away. "Ugh! Scally, you idiot! Get up!" No longer restraining himself, he yanked his small son up to his feet.

Scally was still mostly comatose. "I'm in the bathroom, Pop. Be right out," he hazily relied.

The older man gave his son a good shake. "You're in the living room," he growled.

Chapter 3
The Hulkster & Highlights

As disastrous as the previous night had been, Joey woke the next morning feeling better about his future. Not only was his next match on his home turf, but Lou had given everyone a heads up to prepare for something big. If there was a scout coming, Joey definitely wanted to bring his "A" game. And that meant some touch-ups to his appearance. But first he would leap out of bed for a quick workout. Or would he? After deliberating with himself for a whole three and a half seconds, he decided to double down on comfort and curl back under his "Italian Dream" sheets instead. After all, the sheets were in Joeylicious's own likeness, which is to say, his own likeness. Many would find this creepy. Joey, unfortunately, did not.

* * * * *

Three or four hours later - who's counting? - Joey finally crawled out of bed, grabbed his wallet and made his way to the Rite Aid store a few blocks away. He also put on street clothes first. Normally what is understood doesn't need to be discussed, but this is Joey we're talking about. For the record, he usually got dressed before stepping outside. So now outside his apartment but inside the Rite Aid, Joey scanned through the hair dye aisle. Finding the perfect color, he snatched it up. But his grin quickly faded as he caught sight of the price tag on the box. "$9.99?" he cried as if it were the boxes fault for the grave injustice.

Suddenly, a huge figure, twice the size of Joey in both directions, loomed directly behind the struggling wrestler. "Don't worry, Lisch." The eerily familiar voice immediately got his attention. "Uncle Sam will let you write that off."

Always the wise guy, or at least picking up the slack when Scally wasn't around, Joey greeted the figure: "I haven't turned around yet, but I'm sensing you're rather large for an accountant."

"We need to talk," the figure responded, ignoring the crack.

Turning around to force the oversized being into addressing his wit head on, Joey found himself face to face with his own personal hero, Hulk Hogan. From the signature yellow bandana, to the "Hulkamania" T-shirt, the man appeared ready for a televised match.

"Hulk Hogan?" a stunned Joey could only manage to say, pointing out the obvious.

"In the flesh, brother."

His mind raced trying to catch up with this incredible stroke of luck. "You shop in Rite Aid, too?! I figured you'd be looking into hair plugs before dealing with those not so golden locks." Even with his idols, Joey didn't always make the best first impression.

And clearly not appreciating that fact, Hogan retorted with a quick jab to Joey's face. Joey reeled, falling hard onto the floor. He grabbed his nose in an effort to pinch the blood from pooling out. "What? Can't take constructive criticism?" he pouted. "All I meant was, why do a brand new paint job on an '84 Camaro?" Not a great second impression either.

Hogan bounced off the aisle and brutally delivered onto Joey his signature "leg drop." "Are you ready to shut up and listen to what I have to say?"

Groaning from the floor, the not so young but aspiring wrestler clearly was and was not. "I'm in too much pain to talk."

Hogan gave a satisfied nod as he straightened. "Good. Now get your ass up." Folding his arms across his chest, he waited for the Italian Dream to find his footing, which took a lot longer than it should have.

"I'm here to take you under my wing," Hogan finally stated with steely-eyed determination.

Joey gasped, unable to believe what he just heard. "You mean like your pradagi?!"

"Did those highlights seep into your brain? Protege," Hogan shouted back. "To be even clearer so a simple minded fellow like yourself can understand: I want to be your mentor."

Clearing his head, Joey pumped a victory fist before opening his mouth again. When he was sure he wouldn't say anything else stupid, he proclaimed: "This is the greatest day of my life!"

Hogan tried another approach. "You need a change of pace, Lisch. Can you act? My career didn't take off til I was Thunderlips in Rocky III."

"I played Kenickie in Grease at my sixth grade talent show," Joey offered.

"What place you come in?"

"Eighth."

"How many competitors?" the Hulkster pried further.

"Including me?" Joey reflected, but he already knew his answer wouldn't be great. "Seven."

"That math just doesn't work out for you, brother."

"Whatta you know about acting?" Joy shot back feeling his pride wounded. "Siskel and Ebert didn't exactly give Suburban

Commando two thumbs up. I think they gave it the finger!" Okay, that qualified as something else stupid.

After smartening up Joey again, this time with a double overhead chop to the skull, Hogan finished off the would-be-wrestler with a body slam.

Behind them, at the opposite end of the aisle, an elderly African-American woman looked on not entirely sure how to react to the violence taking place.

Joey still hoped to salvage his once in a lifetime encounter. "Hulkster, can you hurry up with this mentorship?" he groaned. "I'm starting to lose consciousness."

Taking pity on his chosen student, Hogan leaned over and helped him to his feet. But as Joey stood up ready to thank his hero for the assistance, something caught his eye. "Holy crap!"

"What is it?" Hogan peered for what had caused such a reaction.

"Anne-Marie Degrassi! She was in love with me in the seventh grade!"

"The lady behind the register?"

They both watched as the reasonable attractive, female cashier who looked about Joey's age dealt with a customer.

Hogan nodded his approval. "She's cute."

"You should've seen her in the seventh grade," Joey reminisced.

"Why would I look at her when she was in the seventh grade? I was a grown man then."

"I'm just trying to give you a frame of reference, Hulkster. You don't have to get so technical."

"You didn't know she worked here?" Hogan pressed.

Shocked at the inclination, Joey vigorously shook his head. "No, I'm not a stalker!"

"Who said anything about that?"

WRESTLING WITH JOEYLICIOUS

Joey stared at Anne-Marie. "My mom usually buys my hair dye, but she's pissed about the wall," he said in an effort to break things down. Naturally, this explanation caused more confusion than enlightenment.

"You have a guilty conscious, Lisch."

"Hey, she was in love with me, alright?"

"You're mom?" Again Hogan was perplexed.

Joey grimaced at the suggestion. "No, Anne-Marie! And, yes, my mom. But in a different way- Jesus, Hulkster, get with it here!"

"I'm with it plenty. Go talk to her."

It was Joey's turn to be confused. "Who? My mom?"

"No, Anne-Marie," Hogan responded with one of his no-nonsense looks.

"Right. But what do I say?"

"Just reintroduce yourself, and see where it leads," the Hulkster offered, keeping it simple. "But be cool about it. Don't be asking if she still carries the torch for you, or if she has a fella. She'll file a restraining order faster than you can pay for that Loreal."

That strategy sounded much easier than it was. At least in Joey's mind. "Can't you come up there with me?" he asked, hoping for a little backup from his mentor.

"No, that's out of my purview."

"Purv-what? I feel like I need a dictionary when I talk to you." You would never know English was Joey's first and only language.

Instead of explaining what he meant, Hogan just grabbed his failing student and shoved him forward. Joey reached Anne-Marie just as her customer took his change and left. He tried to act casual. "Anne-Maire Degrassi," he conversely shouted like a loon.

~ 21 ~

WRESTLING WITH JOEYLICIOUS

An expression of confusion crossed the cute cashier's face. "Cliff?"

Joey was taken aback, immediately jealous of any member of the male species who Anne-Marie may or may not have been friendly with. "Who's Cliff?"

Anne-Marie's eyes went wide as she covered her mouth. "Oh, my God!" Pulling her hands away, she looked him up and down. "Joey Cassata! I didn't recognize you with those highlights."

Not ready to let go of her initial response, Joey remained suspicious. "So for the record, Cliff's not important to you?"

Still in shock at seeing her old flame, Anne-Marie seemed happy for the reunion. "How are you?! It's been like 30 years!"

At that, Joey finally threw all doubts aside. "Yeah, crazy, right?" he beamed. "I'm still wrestling and all, so things are good. Can I get your new phone number?" This was the clearest definition of jumping the gun.

Anne-Marie laughed. "Wow, do you work that fast in the ring?"

"Actually, I rely more on my strength than speed. C'mon, let me take you out! I'm free every night this week. During the day, too." A wall never stopped Joey from achieving his goals. Just ask Scally.

She shook her head. "I'm not. I'm the manager here. Just helping with the register cause the new girl called in sick."

He pushed down his disappointment, and remained cheerful. "Management! Nice! So stock in the company? The works?"

"Not exactly."

"A huge opportunity just presented itself to me as well." Joey looked behind him almost conspiratorially. "Hulkster, you sure you don't wanna pop out and say hello?"

Anne-Marie looked past Joey with curiosity. "Who are you

~ 22 ~

WRESTLING WITH JOEYLICIOUS

talking to?"

When Hogan didn't come out, Joey dismissed it. "Never mind. Hey, you remember the Halloween dance? Sister Marie had to keep separating us during the slow songs."

The smile on the manager's face faded. "You went to the Halloween dance with Rebecca Rizzo."

Joey felt foolish. "I meant our graduation dance," he corrected himself with equal clumsiness.

Anne-Marie's faded smile was now a frown. "No, that was Stacy Alonzo."

He fumbled for another instance that could possibly have been Anne-Marie. "Scally's block party?"

"Jennifer Carazzi." Her smile suddenly reappeared. "You were a popular guy back then," she poked fun with a twinge of sarcasm.

Glad that she didn't seem as upset as he was, Joey shrugged it off. "Yeah, I guess I was. But you and me: that was special. You must be married now. That's the roadblock here, isn't it?"

Anne-Marie gave him a stunned look, but Joey mistakenly took that as an invitation to keep going. "I can sense you still have feelings for me-" That did it.

A familiar voice once again interrupted his shopping: "Restraining order!"

Before Joey could even react, Hogan took him down with a flying clothesline. Joey smashed into a cardboard display advertising on-sale Hershey bars, and the elderly African-American Woman stood just off to the side shaking her head at the scene. She looked down at the Italian nut job. "Forget the hair dye, and chocolate bars; you should be shopping for medication."

The old woman put her stuff down and headed for the door. Joey sat up dazed. His mentor was nowhere to be seen.

~ 23 ~

"Hulkster," he called out. "Where'd you go? Does this mean I won't be your pradagi?"

Anne-Marie hurried to the edge of the counter and looked at her long ago ex with concern in her eyes. "Joey, are you having a seizure? Should I call someone?"

Chapter 4

Fr. Randazzo & Tighty Whities

Joey sat uncomfortably at the table with his mother and Scally. His mother was being unusually quiet as she glared at his best friend. "Joey, why is this person in my kitchen?" she asked, finally speaking up.

Scally opened his mouth. "I-"

"Don't," Joey interrupted. He knew where that misbegotten response was heading. Then he looked into his mother's soul. "Scally has been my best friend, and most loyal supporter since forever."

This was also clearly the wrong approach. "And look where that's gotten you," his mother shot back.

Undeterred, Joey pressed on. "We had our first class, served our first mass, and saw our first match together." Surely that worked because older people loved to be reminded of the good old days. Right?

"Snuka's 'superfly' from the top of the cage, baby," Scally chimed in, unable to help himself.

The two pals gave each other a high five to emphasize the point.

Joey turned back to his mother. "Scally's always been there for me, and now he needs my help... our help."

Mrs. Cassata's eyes widened. "My god, his parents finally threw him out!"

"Let me finish-" Joey began to plead, trying to stem the

damage.

His mother held up her hand. "Don't even say it!"

"Just til he gets back on his feet," Joey pressed further.

Mrs. Cassata looked at her son over her glasses. "He's a fully formed adult, who hasn't been on his feet yet!"

Unable to read the room, Scally added his two cents which turned out to be less than a penny: "I'll stand up right now if that'll settle it."

Nonplussed, Mrs. Cassata ignored the loyal to a fault half wit. She was not about to have Scally-sized holes in every room of the apartment. "He's not staying here."

Joey switched tactics. "Ma, what would Jesus do?" he asked with absolute sincerity.

"Don't gimme that! You haven't been to church since forever."

"He'll sleep in my room."

"You have one bed."

"We'll share."

His mother moaned as she threw up her hands. "Does any part of this conversation get any better?"

Seeing that he was finally getting through to her, Joey tossed in an incentive: "He'll quit drinking."

Taken aback, Mrs. Cassata paused, her eyes shifting to Scally.

"In here," Scally added, pressing his luck.

She wrinkled her nose. "What does that mean?"

"He won't drink in the apartment," Joey explained.

Smelling a rat, Mrs. Cassata glared at both of them. "But he can still drink outside the apartment?"

"Baby steps, Ma. C'mon."

Mrs. Cassata thought on that as Scally literally held his breath. Her cold exterior cracked, but she wasn't about to give

WRESTLING WITH JOEYLICIOUS

in completely without things being on her terms. "I have to be at the lunchroom every morning at seven. The two of you will not keep me up at night! Lights out by 11. Not a minute after."

Surprise and happiness crossed Joey's face. "So he can stay?"

His mother held up a finger signaling that she wasn't finished. "Neither of you will ever miss Sunday dinner!"

"Scal can do that," Joey beamed. "And when have I ever missed Sunday dinner? Best cook in the world! You kiddin' me?"

Scally humbly lowered his head. "Thanks, Mrs. C."

Not quite done yet, she looked between the men who were still children. "One more thing..."

Just from her tone, Joey knew this was going to be a rough ask. Possibly even a deal breaker. He decided it was worth the risk. "Anything! You name it."

That was when the hammer came down. "You get jobs... both of you."

Stunned at first, a wry grin formed on Joey's face. "Ma, I'm a professional wrestler. I make almost 50 bucks an hour before expenses."

His mother wasn't fooled by that logic. She knew exactly how much he "worked." "You wrestle one hour a week."

"I can look into getting my old job back at the bike shop," Scally offered, sensing that he needed to step up his game.

Mrs. Cassata's annoyance turned to the imp. "Didn't you get caught stealing there?" It was a cruel reminder.

Scally wasn't about to give up. "A Schwinn," he elaborated with a coy smile. "I was just borrowing it for a test ride." Borrowing, stealing. Mere semantics.

Done with the excuses and nonsense, Mrs. Cassata waved off Blondie's words. "Do what you have to." Her attention returned to her son. "As for you: we're gonna visit an old friend tomorrow."

"Who?"

She gave him a knowing smile. "Bring your prayer book."

Joey gulped.

* * * * *

Mrs. Cassata marched her son back to a place that was very familiar, but one that Joey had rarely been to in years. At least during the day. Looking around, he couldn't help but feel little had changed. This was Saint Thomas Aquinas, (S.T.A.), Joey's former grammar school and home turf. And, on Saturday night, he would be back to defend it.

His mom headed off to work in the cafeteria which doubled as the gymnasium, so Joey decided he would sneak in a grueling cardio workout while she slung hash. The workout turned out to be a mere two laps around the gym. But, to be fair to the Italian wrestler, his leisurely pace didn't break into a full walk until the second half of the second lap. After all, he did have his standards.

Mrs. Cassata helped prepare the meals in the kitchen, then moved out front to serve them. As always the kids were rowdy and mouthy. The younger kids had already gone through, so she had to deal with the seventh graders. Her least favorite age group, this always made her particularly grumpy. Adjusting her apron, she focused on her work until one of the boys looked displeased with his food.

"Didn't we have this yesterday?"

Mrs. Cassata flashed him a bemused look. "You want variety? Try ordering off the menu."

The boy was honestly surprised. "We have menus?" Clearly

sarcasm was a concept this C minus student was yet to grasp.

Mrs. Cassata waved him on. "Get going!" She dropped a spoonful of mush on his plastic tray, and stared him down until he left. As she watched him go, Mrs. Cassata couldn't help but feel that the future of the planet was in peril. "Is it possible they'll be dumber than my son?" she muttered to herself.

As if the mere mention of her son was enough to summon Joey, he shoved a kid aside and cut the line. Then he smiled at his mom as he held out an empty tray.

Many protests erupted from a chorus of angry seventh graders.

Like her son, Mrs. Cassata entirely ignored them. "You're late," she instead greeted Joey curtly.

Joey nudged his tray closer as if telling his mother not to be cheap with the portions. "Had to finish my cardio," he explained when no portions came forward. "Big match Saturday."

Mrs. Cassata was obviously annoyed, but they had business to attend to. "I'll give you cardio," she grumbled. Then she ripped off her apron. "Clare, take over," she called out to one of her coworkers.

Looking down at his lonely tray, Joey felt his stomach growl. "Can't I eat first?"

Glaring at him over her glasses, Mrs. Cassata let her son know what she thought of his request. She didn't even respond to it. "Let's go."

"I'm hungry," Joey pleaded, almost breaking into tears.

But it was no use. Finally caving, Joey put down his tray and trotted off after his mother, who was a lot faster than she had any right to be. He was almost out of breath by the time he caught up to her. And by the time they climbed two flights of stairs and reached an office door, he appeared to have a collapsed lung as he hunched over huffing and puffing.

Mrs. Cassata paid Joey's athletic shortcomings no mind. What was behind the office door was the paramount issue at hand. And Joey suddenly became aware of that fact. He straightened nervously as his mother knocked. Behind this door was the possibility of a job that had absolutely nothing to do with wrestling. A real job. What could be more frightening? An ominous voice answered the knock, and Mrs. Cassata opened the door for her son. Joey entered like a house pet being dragged through the threshold of a veterinarian office.

Sitting behind the desk that Joey knew was for the principle of the school was a familiar face, though he was clearly a lot older then when Joey had last seen him. His warm brown hair was entirely white now, but Father Randazzo had managed to keep most of it. It had the calming effect of a tame cloud as he peeked up from his paperwork. Diplomas and framed photos of students and faculty hung about as if he was just as proud of the people who had passed through the school as he was of his degrees.

When he saw who had entered, the priest was pleasantly surprised. "Well, well!.."

Joey was relieved. For whatever reason, he had expected to see the same evil nun occupying the office who had occupied it when he was as kid. Sister Marie doled out Nazi like punishment with sinister precision. Like when Scally blew up a toilet in the girls' bathroom with an M-80. Of course, Joey was his unwitting accomplice. Or when Joey refused to cut his long flowing hair that went past his shirt collar. Jesus had long hair, so why couldn't he? Somehow that logic didn't work on the nun. Scally's illogical excuse for blowing up the toilet didn't work much either. As Joey continued to reflect, he did the math and concluded that the old battle axe must have been six feet under by then. And good riddance. But he never thought in a million years that her replacement would be Fr. Randazzo. This priest was actually cool. He was even a mentor to Joey back in the day. He offered guidance to Scally as well, but that project was aborted in the crib. "Father Randazzo?.. You're the principle now?"

The friendly priest smiled as he stood up. "For almost 20 years, Joseph. If you would only come to mass."

Joey felt a moment of shame as he looked down. He had been through this endless times with his mother. "I know, Father. I lost my way." It no longer worked on mom, but Joey hoped that the explanation would be enough to placate the priest.

"Maybe we can help you find it." Fr. Randazzo opened his arms and Joey happily gave his old friend a hug.

"No grabbing my ass now, Padre. Mom's in the room," Joey joked, feeling much better about things.

He was pleased to see the priest laugh, even if it seemed a bit forced. Clearly, his mother didn't find the joke nearly as funny. Giving Joey a hard smack upside his head, Mrs. Cassata glared at him as he ducked away from another potential blow.

"What? I'm kidding!"

"Not funny," she said, in no mood for his antics.

Hoping to restore the peace, Fr. Randazzo held up his hands. "Alright, alright, so what can I do for you two?"

Mrs. Cassata kept her disapproving gaze on Joey. "My son needs a job, Father. Janitor, something in the lunchroom-"

The priest immediately shook his head. "I don't think the lunchroom is a proper place for a wrestler."

"That's what I've been saying," Joey declared triumphantly, as if that settled the argument he and his mother had been having since birth.

Not ready to give up so easily, Joey's mom pressed the

kindly priest further: "These are tough times for him, Father. Anything... please." She knew if she left it up to her son, he would never get a real job. He was a full time dreamer to the end.

Instead of focusing directly on the request, Fr. Randazzo looked his former pupil over. "You know, I caught one of your matches not too long ago. Very exciting."

Pleasantly surprised by this new wrinkle, Joey was eager to hear specifics. "You're kidding! Which one?"

The priest suddenly frowned. "It was at Saint Agnus around Halloween." He nodded as if confirming his memory of a poor outcome.

Crestfallen, Joey visibly sagged. "Damn, I lost that night." He scratched his head apologetically.

"I believe you fought an Irish gentleman."

"Wait, I fight here this week! You have to come," Joey shouted, seeing a chance to really show what he could do. "I'll hook you up with tickets!" He kept the preordained result to himself. Why spoil a good thing?

"I am the principle, so tickets won't be—"

"Promise you'll be there," Joey pleaded.

"I'll do my best." Fr. Randazzo wanted to support his former student, but he couldn't make any guarantees. Things were getting shaky at Bingo lately, and keeping those disgruntled seniors in check was a painstaking task.

Still, this was enough to encourage the struggling wrestler. "See, ma? This man understands me! Always has. Father, remember the time we went camping with Scally? I was only in the sixth grade, but you still let me practice my wrestling moves on you."

The priest suddenly looked uncomfortable. "Uh..."

Not reading the room, Joey kept on reminiscing. Out loud.

WRESTLING WITH JOEYLICIOUS

"Scally and I didn't have tights, so we got in our underwear."

Frowning, Fr. Randazzo shook his head. "That's not-"

"No, I mean... you showed restraint. You're a priest, me and Scally were altar boys, camping in the woods, no one around-See? You understood me... us. You get boys. I mean, men!"

An uncomfortable silence set in as Mrs. Cassata and the priest looked at each other before turning to an embarrassed Joey. It took a minute, but every once in a while his brain caught up to his mouth.

Finally, Fr. Randazzo felt it was time to fill in Joey's memory gaps. "I remember that story a little differently," he began as gently as he could. With a sigh, the priest recounted exactly what had happened.

* * * * *

Way back in the summer of 1986, the much younger priest had been in charge of a group of students, but it was Joey and Scally who had consumed much of his time and energy. He had pitched their tents away from the others in order to keep the two boys from starting widespread shenanigans that would reverberate throughout the camp.

Enjoying a slight reprieve, Fr. Randazzo sat on a beach chair reading a book with a flashlight, waiting for the next wave of chaos that was bound to erupt from his two primary charges.

As Joey stumbled out of his tent, the priest let out a sigh. The only question was what was it this time?

Joey gave him a goofy grin. "Figure four leg lock. You have to let me try it on you," he slurred.

Looking up from his book, Fr. Randazzo's brown hair moved with the breeze. "You okay, Joseph?" he asked, hoping to diffuse the situation.

"Pile driver then! Scally's too small. I practice on him, it's no challenge."

The priest shook his head. "Go back to sleep. We're fishing first thing."

Moving around and nearly falling over, Joey clearly wasn't interested in listening. "C'mon, father! A suplex, or a body slam at least? None of the kids are ever my size!"

The overgrown sixth grader had managed to get close enough for the priest to catch a whiff of something familiar. He narrowed his eyes. "Joseph, have you been drinking?"

Joey's eyes went wide before he did his best to play that off. "Drinking?.. No. Why would you-" As he continued to steady his sway, his mouth transformed into a large chasm in which a loud belch escaped from. "Why would you ask that?" he pressed forward, refusing to acknowledge what that meant.

Concern spread through Fr. Randazzo as he was certain Joey and Scally hadn't brought any of their own alcohol to the campsite. Short of performing a strip search on the rascals, that just couldn't be the case. Patting down his clothes, he stood up with a sense of panic growing. "Where's my-"

All the confirmation the young priest needed stumbled out of the tent in the form of a 4'6 Robert Scally. He had a flask in hand as he smacked the side of the tent and plowed forward into the dirt, his body going spread eagle. To the priest's horror, all the kid was wearing was a pair of tighty whiteys, but Scally wasn't even remotely embarrassed. "Woo-hoo! I am hammered," the scrawny twerp whooped barely coherently.

Putting on his most disappointed expression, Fr. Randazzo stepped forward. "Robert, you hand me that flask right now!"

Scally pulled the flask to his chest as if it were a favorite toy. "Flask is yours, Father," he slurred under a drunken grin, "soon as I empty it." He laughed impishly before taking a large swig, and continued to laugh as he pushed himself up off the ground.

Fr. Randazzo stepped closer to his charge. "You heard what I said, young man," he reminded even more sternly. "Unless you want your parents to hear about this, you'll hand that over pronto!"

"Parents? We're here to wrestle, Father. Look, I even brought my tights." At this, Scally posed in some very inappropriate ways, particularly given his current attire. He ended his modeling spree by trying a spin that nearly took out one of the tents.

Knowing that he could get in serious trouble, both for what the kids were wearing (or not wearing) and their drunken state, the priest finally charged forward. "Okay, that's it," he barked. Moments like this were usually precursors to finger prints and mug shots.

Scally was prepared to deke out the priest, but hoped it wouldn't come to that. "Joey, take him," he shouted.

A hair away from grabbing Scally, Fr. Randazzo felt someone grab him from behind instead. A wide grin formed on Joey's face as he readied the priest for an "atomic drop." The devastating wrestling move knocked the wind right out of the holy man. With his "opponent" now on the ground, Joey refused to relent and a flying elbow followed suit. Seeing his chance to finally turn the tables on someone larger than himself even though everyone was larger than himself, Scally happily threw himself into the fray.

The scene was absolute mayhem! Fr. Randazzo continuously reached futilely for the flask in Scally's hand even as he was continuously pummeled from all angles. Joey was in heaven. Finally wrestling moves were being performed on someone his own size, maybe even an inch or two taller!

WRESTLING WITH JOEYLICIOUS

By the time a ceasefire was called and the flask was safely returned to its rightful owner, the good priest was battered, bruised, covered in dirt, and more than ready to drag both troublemakers back home to their parents. But this was simply not worth the effort. After angrily sending the equally spent boys off to bed, Fr. Randazzo went to take a well deserved swig from his flask- It was empty. Looking at where the brawl had just occurred, he noticed that there wasn't a single drop of liquor spilled on the ground. Rubbing his forehead, the young priest surmised that Scally at least had one talent of note.

Entering his tent to put away the flask, the holy man poked his head back out to make sure no one was looking. Then he pulled out his emergency supply of Jack Daniels. He was going to sleep soundly that night one way or the other.

* * * * *

Back in the present, Fr. Randazzo finally wrapped up his tale, conveniently leaving out the more lurid details. Joey nodded nonetheless. "Oh, yeah. That's what happened."

Mrs. Cassata shared a relieved look with the priest even though she was still clearly embarrassed by her son. Oh, well. So much for that job. "Thanks for your time, Father. I guess we'll uh..." She grabbed Joey's arm, and started to pull him toward the door.

The good priest waved away her concern. "Don't be silly - both of you. Joseph is still a wonderful athlete, and I have just the position for him!"

Stunned by this response, Mrs. Cassata's mouth fell open. "You do?" she asked, quickly composing herself.

Fr. Randazzo could only smile.

Chapter 5

Obstacle Course of Doom

Pleased with his position as Saint Thomas Aquinas's new resident gym teacher, Joey stood in front of a group of seventh graders. He was assessing them just as much as they were assessing him. For his first day, Joey had chosen to wear his signature wrestling singlet and a whistle that dangled from a thin band around his neck. Scally stood by his side, arms folded across his chest to look more authoritative. Many of the students were already taller than him. Was Scally hired as well by the generous priest? Who could tell? He probably would've just shown up anyway. Unsure what to wear, the undersized adult - if you could call him an adult - sported sweats and a wife beater tank top. You know, the usual. Holding a clipboard, he was clearly the administrator of the two unqualified teachers, but he also wasn't feeling well. It wasn't the cold or the flu, mind you; he had a hangover. The kids either didn't notice or didn't care.

Behind the two teachers was an elaborate obstacle course which mere mortals would normally need days to construct. Somehow Joey and Scally slapped it together in a mere matter of minutes. Several of the students whispered amongst themselves in awe of this spectacle, and Joey grinned in pride at his own handy work.

Scally absorbed it all through the haze and discomfort of his former night's transgressions. "And he gave you the basketball team, too?"

"Gym and basketball," Joey replied. "Not bad, huh?"

"But you don't know anything about basketball."

Joey shrugged. "That's why you're my assistant."

Scally wasn't satisfied. "I'm your assistant in gym. Why don't you be my assistant in basketball?"

"Because I'll never be your assistant in anything," Joey said, glaring at his friend.

Scally took a step back. "Okay, man. No need to get personal." He squeezed his eyes to speed up his recovery time. "I still can't believe they pay us for this."

"It gets better," Joey said just before blowing the whistle. It was time to get the real fun started. "Okay, everyone, settle down!"

Immediately, things began to go off the rails. One of the seventh graders pointed accusingly at Joey. "You're the one who cut the lunch line!"

"I saw him wrestle last week," another one chimed in. "Shamrock kicked his ass!"

Whatever he was going to say to the "line cutting" accusation was quickly lost at the mere mention of the man who had caused him so much pain and humiliation of late. "That name is forbidden in this class henceforth," Joey warned.

Instead of that inspiring fear, one of the other kids just laughed. "Nice uniform, douche. "

The rest of the class joined in on the verbal abuse toward their teacher. Joey blew harder on his whistle, and shot everyone his best villain glare. "Enough! I need your full attention, so no one gets hurt!"

The threat of actual physical harm finally got the class to go quiet.

WRESTLING WITH JOEYLICIOUS

"In front of you stands today's obstacle course," Joey pressed forward. "It's filled with danger and excitement. It'll also teach you something very valuable in the end." He was pleased by his students' sudden change in demeanor, and turned to his assistant. "Line 'em up."

Baffled, Scally looked around. "Where?"

Joey stared deadpan as if it were obvious. "At the starting line."

The ditzy blonde continued to search. "Where's that?"

Exasperated, Joey threw up his hands. "At the begin-" One look at Scally, and he knew that he had to make it impossible for the knucklehead to miss. Scally missed a lot. "There," he finally said, pointing directly at the starting point.

Scally strolled over, turned and gave a big "thumbs up."

Addressing his students, Joey shouted: "Everybody behind Scally - single file!"

As the kids followed their teacher's instruction to the letter, Joey trotted to the other end of the obstacle course. "Scal, they ready?" he hollered.

"Uh... I guess so," his friend replied, not sure what was needed for them to be ready.

"On my mark, send them through one at a time."

Looking down at his clipboard, Scally used his finger to scan the names. "Mark? I have three Matts, but no Marks."

Joey rolled his eyes. "No, not-" Realizing there was no hope in trying to explain what he meant, he shouted: "When I say go, okay?!"

"So send the Matts first?"

"I don't care who you send first! Just send them one at a time!.. Ready?.. Go!"

Deciding it was too much trouble figuring out which ones were the Matts and if there really weren't any Marks, Scally just gave a quick shove to the student closest to the starting area.

The happy-go-lucky kid did a great job making his way through the obstacles. And when he neared the end, he noticed Joey standing at the finish line looking happy as well. This strange being in a wrestling singlet must have just been there waiting to congratulate him for a job well done. Scrambling through the finish line, happy-go-lucky emerged beaming. He wanted to let his teacher know that the course wasn't that difficult, even though he was a little out of breath. Before he could deliver his Yelp rating, though, Joey struck him with a flying clothesline, knocking not so happy-go-lucky clear off his feet.

Back at the other end of the course, Scally continued to send stunned kids through one at a time. They moved increasingly slower through the maze now that they knew what lesson was waiting for them in the end. Regardless of their pace, each student was eventually met with a devastating wrestling move from their new teacher. He was merciless, doling out body slams, drop kicks, flying elbows, anything he could think of to let them know who was boss.

Scally sent the last student through, feeling a little sorry for Stuey. The tiny runt reminded Scally of himself in a way. And, unlike most of the other kids, Stuey even struggled through many of the obstacles.

Joey watched Stuey's progress with devilish delight. Behind him, the other kids were sprawled out on the floor panting from their "lessons" and now Joey was about to deliver the final one. When Stuey finally reached the end, Joey leapt at him, a huge cat-like grin on his face.

Suddenly, Stuey moved much faster than he had during the course. Sidestepping Joey's attack, he watched as his teacher

WRESTLING WITH JOEYLICIOUS

hit the floor splat and then he sprung into further action. He dove on top of the much larger Italian before Joey could even grasp what was happening. Busting out the signature move of his favorite wrestler John Cena, Stuey delivered the "Five Knuckle Shuffle" with utter perfection. The tiny but powerful runt then finished off his wannabe teacher with a vicious submission hold known as the "Stepover Toehold Facelock," (or STF), which was another staple of Cena's. Stuey's heroes were more modern than Joey's heroes, and it showed.

Unable to see from his vantage point what all the commotion was about, Scally dashed to the end of the course. He arrived just in time to see his best friend being tapped out by Joey's first victim who was now playing referee.

Stuey leapt up and held his hands in a victory pose. All the other seventh graders forgot about their crushed pride as they stood and roared their approval for the unexpected twist.

Joey looked up just long enough to witness his own new low before collapsing in humiliation. He was no longer certain that his new ideal job was so ideal after all.

Chapter 6

A Tiny Slam from Glory

After his disastrous day at the office so to speak, Joey could not wait for his next fight. No 85 pound Stueys would get in the way of that preordained win... if he could just lift and slam Tiny. As he entered the S.T.A. locker room in pre-fight attire, tingling with anticipation, Joey made his way to a group of wrestlers clustered around someone he couldn't see. As some of the wrestlers parted for him like the Red Sea, Joey was suddenly face to face with the well-dressed Salvatore Morelli, president of BRAWL. Lou, who was standing next to Morelli, really had been serious. This was definitely cause for everyone to bring their "A" game.

Joey's face brimmed with startled excitement. "Mr. Morelli?"

Morelli, also of Italian decent, turned and took in the new arrival. "You must be the Italian Dream."

"More like the Italian cat nap," Paddy Shamrock muttered as the two fellow Italians shook hands.

"So now you grace us with your presence," Joey shot back, seeing that Shamrock had actually made a locker room appearance for once. "As soon as the President of the league shows up!"

Opening his mouth toward Morelli as if to say something in his defense, the Irish Adonis decided to hold back knowing that the other wrestlers would only take Joey's side.

~ 42 ~

WRESTLING WITH JOEYLICIOUS

"Whatever," he simply replied. With that limp retort, he left. No one was disappointed.

Joey turned back to the big boss. "What brings you here, Mr. Morelli? Scouting for high school venues?"

"Actually, my son goes to this school."

"He does? What grade? I teach gym!" Wait. Maybe Joey shouldn't have mentioned that. He wasn't about to receive glowing referrals from his students just yet. Or ever.

"Second," Morelli answered.

"Cool. I'll uh... make sure I go easy on him."

The president laughed. "Good luck tonight. It's nice to have a fellow Italian to root for." Patting Joey on the back, Morelli headed out toward the gym and the other wrestlers dispersed.

"Thanks, Mr. Morelli," Joey called after him. His excitement now at a crescendo, he turned to Lou who was looking coy. "You hear that, Lou? Fellow Italian! This could be my big break!"

"You never know," Lou said with a knowing smile.

"If I could just slam Tiny…"

On cue, Joey spotted Tiny leaning against his locker devouring an overstuffed meatball hero.

"Damn it, Tiny," the frustrated Italian exclaimed. "You have to eat before the match? Hard enough to pick you up as it is!"

Tiny just gave him a shrug, causing one of the meatballs to wiggle precariously in the sandwich. Then, as he followed the last of the other wrestlers out, the meatball made its escape and exploded on the floor. Tiny gave it no mind.

"Don't you remember WrestleMania III, brother?" a familiar voice announced, startling Joey.

Standing where Lou had just been was suddenly Joey's blonde hero who knew a lot about hair dye prices. "They said no one could slam the Giant," Hulk Hogan continued as if this was a routine occurrence.

"You're right, but that was a bit of a squeaker," Joey responded with equal matter of fact-ness.

"Did I lift him and drop him, or not?"

"You definitely dropped him."

Hogan narrowed his eyes. "Never use sarcasm on your hero... especially when he possesses the ability to rip off your limbs."

Joey wasn't about to back down. "Hulkster, your legs were shaking when you had the Giant up. And didn't you tear something in your back?"

"No one cares about the details! Just slam the man! The Giant was twice the size of Tiny!"

"And you're twice the size of me," Joey shouted back. Unfortunately.

"Then it works out perfectly!" Hogan grabbed Joey by the back of the neck, and repeatedly rammed his head against one of the lockers.

Lou, who had moved to another part of the room, turned toward the disturbance. But it wasn't Hogan who was slamming Joey into the locker; it was Joey slamming himself. Lou continued to watch perplexed as Joey then crashed a chair over his head. There was no one else even near him.

Morelli strolled back in from the gym. "Lou, you need to do something about these pathetic ticket sales-" He never finished that thought, though, as the antics of the Italian Dream immediately caught his attention. "Wow, this guy's really committed to his work!"

Lou shrugged. "He's committed alright. Or should be."

* * * * *

WRESTLING WITH JOEYLICIOUS

The match between Joeylicious and Tiny began like all the rest. First, Tiny was introduced by the announcer who also doubled as the referee due to budgetary constraints. Then Tiny worked the sporadic but boisterous crowd as they howled and threw whatever they could get their mitts on at him. This was followed with the glorious introduction and entrance of Joeylicious! For once the Tower of Power who was too sweet to be sour was not the challenger. Not that he was defending a belt or anything. The only belt Joey or his alter ego owned was from JC Penney. But Joeylicious was the hometown hero to this motley crew of a misfit audience, so he got whatever cheers they could muster. And now the actual wrestling kicked in!

Among the spectators in the S.T.A. gym, which was even smaller than the usual BRAWL venue, was Father Randazzo. He watched with interest, but with none of the other fans' exuberance. Morelli and his eight-year-old son sat a few rows behind the priest with their eyes glued. Little Morelli was especially enthralled with the proceedings. In the row just behind BRAWL's royal family was Scally holding his usual Styrofoam cup of beer. As things in the ring heated up, all parties acted accordingly.

Joeylicious made his way toward his preordained victory, stunning his opponent with chops and kicks that kept Tiny reeling. Facing someone who relied on strength over agility made it easy for the S.T.A. alumni to put on a good show. It was like beating the side of a barn that moved like a melting glacier. Or a barn. Now all Joeylicious had to do was get Tiny in the air. Somehow. He feverishly worked himself up to what he still thought was an impossible feat. The bigger problem was that Tiny was starting to fade, sliding further and further down the ropes with each hit. Joeylicious knew that once Tiny hit canvas, he became canvas.

Fearing that his best friend and favorite wrestler might lose a golden opportunity, Scally jumped to his feet and hopped up and down to egg him on. "C'mon, Joey! Body slam him!"

The words were clear, and for a second, Joeylicious stopped and looked around the gym. This was his home turf, and he just had to deliver!

"Do it, Lisch," Tiny grunted, struggling to remain vertical. "I can't stay up much longer!" As if to prove his point, Tiny fell against the ropes once more and seemed unable to stop his body from continuing its downward slide to the canvas this time.

Realizing that it was now or never, Joeylicious went into desperation mode. He thrust himself under Tiny, and felt for enough flab to get a good grip to actually lift the behemoth. His opponent was slick with sweat, and from this close, the Italian Dream could smell the meatball hero on Tiny's breath. Glad that he would have to hold his own breath to actually slam Tiny, Joeylicious sucked in his gut. With the 300+ pound sweat gland finally in the air, S.T.A.'s own wobbled just like Hulk Hogan did with Andre the Giant at WrestleMania III. This was as precarious as it could get, but Joeylicious had one last burst of energy left. He dug deep - real deep - as deep as he ever had in his entire wrestling career - and slammed Tiny to the canvas with a roaring thud!

The crowd went wild. Scally was so fired up that he even did the unimaginable – he spilled his beer. Of course, the beer went all over Morelli's eight-year-old son.

As if Morelli felt the impact of the beer himself, he immediately looked down at his soaked kid and then leaped up to confront Scally. "You imbecile! You just gave my son a bath!"

WRESTLING WITH JOEYLICIOUS

Still excited, Scally brushed it off. "Relax, gumba! Whattaya gonna whack me now?"

"You have any idea who you're talking to?"

"You seem like a typical greaseball to me," Scally shot back. He was certain this clown was just another fan too big for his britches.

Little Morelli burst into tears.

Scally, now with a new source of entertainment to revel in, spouted to anyone who would listen: "Hey look: the greaseball's kid needs a lesson in manhood!"

"That's it," big Morelli snarled. And with surprising speed and agility, he threw himself at Scally, taking both of them to the floor.

Completely unaware of the fiasco taking place in the bleachers, Joeylicious waited patiently for the ref to do his job. Once he heard the count of three, Joeylicious leapt off the spent behemoth and extended his victorious arms into the air. As he pumped his fists, he couldn't help but to cut his celebration short so he could scan to where the president of BRAWL had been sitting. Fully expecting Morelli's instant approval, Joey's eyes darted back and forth unable to find his salvation.

Then a well-dressed man stood up in the middle of a brawl apparently occurring in the crowd. Worse than that, this same well-dressed man was apparently pounding on a very familiar scrawny figure.

"No... no," Joey muttered before dashing under the ropes and making his way toward the mayhem, hoping all along that he was hallucinating. He arrived just in time to see Morelli and Scally getting pulled apart, with the president clearly coming out the winner. Like laser beams, Joey's furious eyes locked in on his soon to be former best friend. "Scally, you idiot!"

~ 47 ~

WRESTLING WITH JOEYLICIOUS

Fr. Randazzo had managed to sneak away from the ruckus before it got out of hand. Knowing how things would end, though, the good priest could only shake his head in disappointment as he made his way toward the exit.

Morelli turned his anger toward Joey. "You know this guy?"

Too late. Joey realized his mistake. Trying to backpedal, he shook his head. "No, no, why would you- I never saw him before."

"You just called him by name!"

Misreading the looks Joey was throwing at him for an attempted bailout, Scally cozied up to his pal. "Me and Joe are best buds! What's it to you, greaseball?"

Morelli motioned for security. "Get him outta here!"

Two large security guards grabbed Scally and carried him toward the exit. One guard would have easily been enough.

Scally was stunned. "Hey, what'd I do?" he bemoaned. "Joe, talk to these guys, will ya?! Let me down!"

With one problem out of the way, Morelli turned back to Joey. "And you have yourself a nice career." The president gave a quick move of his hand, and two more security guards moved in. Grabbing Joey, they escorted him toward the exit as well.

"Wait, Mr. Morelli! I won," Joey yelled, panicking over his complete reversal of fortune. Like a squiggly eel, he struggled to break free from the men hauling him away.

It was no use.

Several other security guards joined in on Joey's removal, including one familiar looking one with thinning blonde locks. As Joey was lifted into the air to prevent him from gaining any traction, the Italian Dream continued to plead with the president: "You were gonna bump me up to high school venues! I'm Italian!"

WRESTLING WITH JOEYLICIOUS

With a mocking smile, Morelli waved at the wrestling peasant before turning his attentions to his son. After watching his father beat up the loser who had soaked him with beer, little Morelli was far less upset.

Thinning blonde locks continued to assist security with Joey. "Your big break, huh?" he chided his middle-aged "pradagi."

Knowing he was defeated, Joey sagged. "Tell me about it-" But then he quickly realized who was making fun of him. "Hulkster, you're in on this?! This place has more security than fans!"

Hulk Hogan flashed him a knowing smile. "We'll straighten you out. Eventually."

Confused, Joey looked around to see who or what Hogan was referring to. "Eventually?! Who's we?!"

Hogan simply laughed as the aspiring wrestler was finally hauled through the threshold of the exit sign.

Chapter 7

The True Cost of Priceless

Battered and beaten, both bodily and spiritually, Joey and Scally limped home from their grammar school alma mater. Although Joey was victorious in the ring, outside the ropes had been a colossal disaster. If the humiliation of getting eighty-sixed by security wasn't bad enough, Father Randazzo had been waiting for his two resident gym teachers outside in the school parking lot. And after a frank discussion, Saint Thomas Aquinas was now down one of their resident gym teachers. Scally, drowning his sorrows with a 40 ounce bottle of whatever battery acid he could legally or illegally carry inside a brown paper bag, made it crystal clear which of the two would be sleeping in late come Monday morning.

"How do you let Father Randazzo fire me, and not quit gym teachin' yourself?" Scally muttered, his lips as close to a pout as he could manage. It was as if he thought the bag concealing his 40 ounce was also masking the reason for so many of his woes.

Joey, fighting the urge to point out the obvious, looked over at his troubled and troubling friend. "Because you, not me, instigated that brawl with Morelli!" So much for fighting that urge. "Why do you have to get your ass kicked in the bleachers all the time?"

Even if Scally's stock was down - way down - about as down as one's stock could get - and it was - he was still not out. And

WRESTLING WITH JOEYLICIOUS

him not being out meant that he could still be a wisenheimer when properly called upon. "You get your ass kicked in the ring; it's the least I could do."

Joey could only sigh because he had actually won the night's fight after pulling off the impossible – lifting and slamming the massive wrestler ironically named Tiny. "Well, this fiasco cost me my life insurance policy. I had to donate it to the league just to stay in it."

Scally laughed as if that shouldn't have been a problem at all. "I was banned from your corner three years ago! Never stopped me from comin' each week."

"I'm in real danger now," Joey shouted, frustrated by his manager's inability to grasp his plight. "All my opponents have a motive to kill me for real in the ring!"

Scally dismissed that with a shrug. "Karma's a bitch."

Thankfully, they had reached their destination. Home. Another quarter of a block, and Joey would've surely negotiated a piledriver between his idiot friend and the concrete. But as Joey and Scally climbed the stairs that led to the Cassata apartment, that piledriver was suddenly looming once more. Scally reminded his larger friend of this fact when he reached for the apartment's doorknob with one hand, while cradling his 40 ounce bottle with the other.

Joey grabbed him. "Whoa, whoa! Where do you think you're going?"

"What?! You're evicting me now, too?" Scally replied incredulously.

"You know the rule," Joey shot back, "no drinking inside the apartment!"

There was horror in the lush's eyes as he looked down at his brown paper bag. "Joe, this is a 40!"

"I don't care! You drink that out here, or you throw it away!"

WRESTLING WITH JOEYLICIOUS

It was easily the hardest decision of Scally's not so short life. His gaze moved back and forth between the bottle and the door. On the one hand he wanted to get inside and crash. On the other hand, it was, as he pointed out, a 40.

In no mood to watch his drunken friend go through the long list of pros and cons, Joey shook his head and entered the apartment that his mother mostly paid for. Well, more than mostly. "Completely" would be the more appropriate adverb. Unconcerned with his contribution to the rent, though, he just shut the door. Scally was left behind like a wounded soldier on the battlefield. Only his wound came from shooting himself.

A mere 30 seconds passed before Joey, out of the kindness of his heart or just pity, reopened the door. Scally, minus the 40 now, was completely blitzed and sprawled out on the floor. Joey kicked the bottom of his shoes. When that had no effect, he leaned over and in a low voice threatened to practice his latest wrestling moves on the nearly unconscious blonde. For a second, the Irish-American shot up, his fists ready to fight. But a goofy smile quickly spread across his face as he saw who his opponent would be.

Finally sick of the games, Joey hoisted Scally to his feet, pointed him in the right direction and let go. Like a youngster learning how to ride a bike without training wheels for the first time, Scally stumbled through the door.

"Be careful, will you?" Joey hissed.

"I don't make the rules; I follow 'em," Scally slurred back, somehow still standing. He tried to turn and look at Joey as if what he said was actually funny, but his arms flailed. He grabbed onto an expensive looking, glass dog statue for support.

Quickly moving forward, Joey tried to stop his friend from using the objects around them as disposable props for his

WRESTLING WITH JOEYLICIOUS

drunken antics. "Don't touch that! My mom bought it in Italy! It's priceless!"

The words were lost on his best friend and manager, though, as Scally's eyes tried to absorb what they were seeing. His index finger reached out and tapped the glass dog on the nose. "Since when are you allowed pets in here?"

When it didn't move, Scally frowned at the pet, perhaps realizing that it wasn't alive. Trying to cover for his drunkenness, he then straightened to look the unanimated object in the eyes. Big mistake. By straightening, he needed to push off the glass statue, which immediately led to it falling off its pedestal.

Joey watched as if everything happened in slow motion. For a fraction of a second, it looked like the statue might not respond to gravity. But, as Joey had found so many times in the ring, there was no way to defy the laws of Sir Isaac Newton for long. The statue succumbed to the pull, and made its inevitable way to the floor.

It was only when the dog statue reached the floor that time seemed to resume at its usual pace. This came with the sound of the glass shattering into a thousand pieces. Joey blinked and when his eyes opened, his mother's prized possession was unrecognizable. Instead of a dog, it looked more like the Honky Tonk Man's guitar after it was smashed over "Macho Man" Randy Savage's head during their 1987 Intercontinental Championship match.

"Joey!" The call from the other room happened before Joey could fully digest what he had just witnessed. His mother's voice was even louder than the smashing of the glass.

His mind cycling through a wealth of scenarios, Joey scrambled for an explanation that wouldn't lead to Scally getting kicked out of the apartment. This was going to take some magic. If only he could delay the inevitable confrontation til the next day: the mandatory Sunday night dinner.

* * * * *

Of course, the tension hung in the air all through the night, the next morning and the next afternoon. Only Scally seemed immune to it, largely because he had little recollection of what had happened. As promised, both Joey and Scally were present for their mandatory Sunday dinner. Not that Joey had wished to miss it. He loved his mother's Sunday feasts: the spaghetti and meatballs, the sausage and manicotti - Fuhgeddaboudit! Whatever she made was perfectly delicious. And this time, she really outdid herself - a clear sign that she was not happy. When she was upset, Mrs. Cassata cooked. Since Scally had moved in, Joey had gotten accustomed to eating more than he had any right to.

Yes, Joey and his mother were well aware of the high stakes at this possible last supper, but the source of the ill will was obliviously stuffing his face. Deciding it was time for Scally to face the music, Mrs. Cassata cleared her throat to demand the scrawny devourer's attention. She would at least make him as miserable as he made her. "New amendment to the rule: either you get yourself cleaned up entirely, or you're outta this apartment."

Even though he was looking right at her when she said it, Scally seemed surprised. So much so, he didn't bother to finish chewing his food as he pointed his fork at himself. "Talkin' to me?"

Grinding her teeth, Mrs. Cassata narrowed her eyes. "Do you have any idea how much that statue cost?"

WRESTLING WITH JOEYLICIOUS

Scally pointed the blame at her son, a bit of sauce dripping onto the table from his fork. "Joey said it was priceless."

"It was," she growled, with her eyes now on the newly formed sauce stain.

"So then how did it cost anything?"

"You get yourself in a program." Mrs. Cassata leaned forward. "I'm serious." She was just getting started as her attention shifted from one problem to another. Her son. "As for you..."

Startled, Joey's eyes widened. "What 'as for me?' I'm working for the school now, I'm here for Sunday dinner—"

His mother's finger immediately came out, and Joey knew what that meant. She was going to broach the one subject that made him wince. Well, one of the subjects that made him wince. There were many such subjects. "When are you giving me a grandchild?! I mean, are you even dating?"

"I'm focused on the wrestling! Fame and fortune there, and the ladies follow." Joey's response was clearly logical. To him anyway.

"Ask me if I'm holding my breath," his mother retorted, shooting down such delusions of grandeur.

Now Joey's eyes narrowed, but he knew better than to verbalize anything else. Instead, he just glared.

But the glare he gave his mother was immediately undermined by the only non-Italian at the table. "Are ya holdin' your breath, Mrs. C? That's probably bad for digestin' the manigot."

Unaccustomed to anyone interrupting discussions about her son's future, Mrs. Cassata threw in the towel. In an attempt to mask her frustration, she rose and brought her dish to the sink. With his mom thrown off by Scally's latest innocent, albeit dumb remark, Joey quickly finished eating and dragged his friend out of the apartment before she regained her composure.

Knowing that they had dodged a bullet, Joey kept Scally out until late that night. When he was certain his mom had gone to bed, he retired to his own with Scally. Yes, they really were sleeping in the same bed. With Scally fast asleep, snoring like a bear with laryngitis, Joey stared at the ceiling contemplating his future. There was a lot to consider. First, he had to get Scally to take things seriously. It was only a matter of time before his mom would bring up her desire for grandchildren again, and his wrestling career was on the ropes. But Scally was easily the most pressing problem. If he could get that straightened out, there wouldn't be anything to distract him from his goals. Rolling over, an image of Anne-Marie passed through his head. He mumbled something about her as he drifted off to sleep.

Chapter 8
10 or 15% of Anne-Marie

The next day, Joey took his best friend and worst enemy out for another walk. He couldn't exactly wrestle Scally into submission, but it was time to buckle down and play his mom's role at least. Of course, things got off to a rocky start when the blonde menace took a swig from a hidden flask.

"You better listen to my mom," Joey said, reacting in frustration.

Taking offense, Scally held up the flask. "Look how small this is! At least I'm cuttin' back."

"How many times you refill that today, and it's not even noon?"

"Semantics," Scally muttered.

Feeling he had tried to be reasonable, Joey resorted to his preferred method of persuasion. "Bush club!"

Before Scally could react, Joey had already shoved him. And hard. Unwilling to drop his flask and unable to grab onto anything with his free hand, he went tumbling into a row of well-manicured shrubs. Landing upside down, Scally blinked up at his friend in confusion. Like a fish out of water, he squirmed. "I'm stuck!"

Feeling guilty, but not really, Joey leaned over and lifted the imp out of the bushes. Scally, brushing his clothes and pulling twigs and leaves out of his hair, knew when it was time to change the subject. "So why didn't you bring up Anne-Marie

WRESTLING WITH JOEYLICIOUS

Degrassi to your mom?"

Joey looked away. "I told you about that Rite Aid disaster."

"I heard she's back on the market. And she has a kid!"

This was news to Joey. "Really? We didn't get to the kid part in our discussion."

"Yeah, a little girl," Scally added.

Joey considered his options as his friend continued to clean himself up. Believe it or not, Scally's words were actually sinking in. "Wait, she's divorced?!"

Scally shook his head as he threw the last leave back into the bushes. "She's a widow. Her husband died in a bizarre jump-roping accident."

The one day a week wrestler took pause. Was this the world's first death by jump-roping?

"Some guy from outta town," Scally continued. "He was exercising outside, tripped on the rope and hit his head on a curb or something. What an idiot!"

Joey dismissed the odd detail to the even odder event. It really didn't hurt or help his chances with Anne-Marie either way. New hope was beginning to form in his mind. Their initial reunion hadn't been great. Far from it. He had obliterated a sales display of chocolate bars right in front of Anne-Marie's eyes. But this new bit of news changed everything. She was a young widow with a child. Joey felt certain that he would come off as the good guy, opening up his home and heart to her. And then she would remember just how much she loved him. Things were falling into place.

"You could stop by the store again," Scally said excitedly, his words cutting into Joey's musings.

With this one sentence, all of Joey's pleasantries suddenly crash-landed. "That's the last place I'm stopping by! Besides, Anne-Marie is still married in the eyes of our Lord." Of course.

WRESTLING WITH JOEYLICIOUS

Why didn't he think of that sooner? This was the way he always talked himself out of positive steps forward in life.

Scally quickly dismissed that load of bunk. "Well, when she reaches the Lord, she can rekindle her marriage. In the meantime, she's a package deal with the daughter. Your mom's 'grandchild' problem solved."

There was a real simplicity to that logic; Joey had to admit. He reflected with a smile. "Ahhh, Anne-Marie DeGrassi... Remember our seventh grade field trip - how much she was into me?"

An equally happy expression passed over Scally's face as he thought about that same memory. "Ahhh, how could I forget?"

This quickly brought Joey back into the present and his eyes narrowed. His feelings about that day were just as fresh after three decades. And they weren't all good. "Yeah, how could you?!"

* * * * *

That particular day back in the seventh grade had started off so promising. Their class had gone on a field trip to a dude ranch, and Joey had been one of the more popular students. Still dwarfing all the other kids in both size and strength, he looked around the barn where they were ending their day's activities. The animals in their pens were hardly the focus of the budding teenagers at that moment, though.

All the adults were out of sight, and the sound of one of the boys letting out a battle cry was music to Joey's ears. Turning to his classmates, he was ready to put on a show - especially for the girls standing off to the side. The boys reached him one at a time, making it all too easy to take them down with a wide range of devastating wrestling moves.

~ 59 ~

WRESTLING WITH JOEYLICIOUS

Scally stood rooting for his pal amongst the girls, who all giggled over the impressive athletic display. He turned to look at young Anne-Marie DeGrassi and the adoring expression on her face as she watched the heroics. Scally's eyes shifted back to Joey, and he began to fantasize about the women who would be interested in the manager of a famous wrestler some day.

"Boys, enough," a young woman shouted, storming into the barn. Her presence alone was more than enough to stop the rascals' antics, mostly because of how attractive she was. They were all putty in Miss Whalen's hands when it came right down to it.

The only one to ignore her was Joey, who was much more interested in his next opponent than his teacher. Finishing a final suplex on the closest boy, he finally looked up with a huge grin.

The exasperated expression on Ms. Whalen's face caused the smile on the young wrestler to falter. "Joey, please... before you kill someone."

Scally strolled over to his pal, quick in his attempt to deflect her concerns. "It's okay, Miss W. All the parents signed waivers."

The wry look she flashed let the little troublemaker know that she was about to burst his bubble. "They signed permission slips. And permission to fight was not granted."

Scally still sensed an opportunity to show off his managerial skills. "Well, you know, I organized all this." He gave her the most charming look he could muster. In reality, Scally looked rather sleazy for a seventh grader. "Maybe you should keep me after school."

"We aren't at school today," Ms. Whalen responded with complete deadpan.

"You could take me into the barn and scold me."

WRESTLING WITH JOEYLICIOUS

"Get on the bus, Robert." No longer interested in his foolishness, the teacher looked around at the rest of the class. "And that goes for everyone! It's time to head home!"

A collective groan sounded as if she were trying to herd the farm animals out of the barn. The students then grumbled amongst themselves as they headed to the bus.

Seeing a unique opportunity, Joey worked his way toward the prettiest girl in class. Anne-Marie could see him working his way toward her, so she made sure to hang back away from her girlfriends.

The grin on his face hid Joey's uncertainty. His heart beating like a jack rabbit, he tried to exude confidence. "So what'd you think?"

He needn't have worried, though, as Anne-Marie turned her large eyes toward him in admiration. "That was amazing!"

Hearing that, Joey decided to really lay it on thick. He looked back toward the barn. "Yeah, I took it easy on 'em. I save my most vicious moves for adults."

Giving him a shy look, Anne-Marie still wanted to keep Joey's attention. She knew how quickly he could get distracted by the other girls, who were just as eager to talk to him after he wrestled as she was. Remembering she had something to share, she pulled her bookbag around and took out a pack of pink Sno Ball cakes her mother had packed for her that morning. She thrust one of them toward Joey.

His mouth salivated at the sight of the marshmallowy treat, and he reached for it. When his fingers brushed the palm of Anne-Marie's hand during the transfer, she began to blush. "Aren't these delicious?" she asked, distracting herself from her thoughts.

Joey had just taken a bite, but he wanted to respond in a way that was cool. Shoving the cake to the side of his mouth, he smiled. "Well, I am vicious and-" His eyes went wide. "Wait a minute! Say that again!"

Confused, she looked down at her Sno Ball. "Delicious?"

"Vicious and delicious..." He mused. "Yeah, I like the sound of that!"

Clueless to what Joey was going on about, Anne-Marie was more concerned about keeping his focus on her. "Can I sit next to you on the bus?"

The suddenness of the question brought Joey back to reality. As interested as he was in her, Joey didn't want her getting the wrong idea. "Listen, Anne-Marie... no disrespect or anything, but I'm not looking to settle down til I'm Champ."

Her shoulders slumped as she stared at her partially eaten dessert.

Feeling a bit guilty, he offered her a fair consolation: "But I'm cool with making-out on the ride home."

Her eyes lit up. "Okay!"

They boarded the bus together and moved toward the back. One look from Joey and the two boys occupying the last seat quickly got up and moved to another part of the bus.

Anne-Marie bounced as she sat, her excitement getting the better of her. Joey sat down beside her, his voice lower than usual as he began to flirt.

As it got darker outside, Joey removed his jacket. Holding it up, he leaned over to kiss Anne-Marie. Her lips were puckered up, and she sat stiffly as he got close. Laughing, he gave her a quick peck on the lips.

Moments later, Joey had warmed up, and the kisses got more intense. He peeked out to make sure they weren't in danger of getting caught, and was pleased to see Ms. Whalen talking animatedly with the bus driver up front. Chuckling to himself, he turned his attention back to Anne-Marie. He felt a twinge

WRESTLING WITH JOEYLICIOUS

of pity for Scally because Whalen clearly had a thing for the driver, but that quickly left his mind. Making out with his girl of the moment, Joey was certain there would be no more interruptions.

As things got hot and heavy, at least in seventh grade terms, Anne-Marie pulled away slightly and giggled. "Joey, stop..."

Joey moved closer and gave her another deep kiss. "What? You don't like my technique?" he finally responded.

She looked at him shyly "No, the kissing is fine. It's your hands."

Confused, Joey looked at her. "I'm not using my hands."

Her expression shifted, and Anne-Marie looked annoyed. "I'm not kidding..."

Realizing there was something more sinister at play, Joey removed his jacket that was acting as a blanket for them. Smiling up at him was Scally, his scrawny right hand hidden up Anne-Marie's shirt.

"Scally, you idiot," Joey yelled, swinging at the perverted runt.

Moving out of reach, Scally held up his hands. "Lisch, I'm your manager. I get 15%."

"10%!"

"That's an agent!"

"And an ass-kicking!" Joey wasn't about to let someone weasel in on his girl. Scally had gone too far, and he was going to teach him a lesson about what he was willing to share - signed contract or not.

Amazingly, neither Ms. Whalen nor the bus driver noticed or cared as Joey began to throw his best friend around the back of the bus like a rag doll. The other kids cheered at the impromptu entertainment.

WRESTLING WITH JOEYLICIOUS

* * * * *

Remembering that day still upset Joey, and he hovered over his now adult friend back in the present. Without a word, he shoved Scally back into the shrubs and walked away.

Again Scally blinked at the sudden change in perspective, his body hanging upside down with his head just a couple of inches off the ground. "C'mon, Lisch! That's ancient history," he called out in desperation. "You're still carryin' that around?"

But Joey would not be lending a helpful hand this time.

Scally wiggled frantically. "I'm really stuck this time... Help!"

Chapter 9

Golden God & Asian Goddesses

Scally looked up at the ominous building and sighed. He was only there because his best friend's mom had threatened to kick him out of the apartment, and he knew it. The scrawny tornado would have been fine living his life as poorly as ever, but, alas, it was not to be the case. With another sign, he entered the building's facility and approached the receptionist.

She looked to be about the same age as Mrs. Cassata, and the stern glare of her arresting green eyes made Scally feel sheepish. "May I help you?" The receptionist's tone was more of a demand than a question.

Scally managed to steady himself. "Yes, I have a problem."

She forced a smile. "Then you've come to the right place." The receptionist was clearly waiting for Scally to rattle off more specifics, but he wasn't ready to elaborate just yet.

The sound of the entrance door opening behind him was a welcome distraction, and Scally turned to see two attractive Asian women enter the facility. They didn't stop by the receptionist. Instead, they continued to walk straight to the back, turning only when they reached the room at the end of the hall.

Almost as if being woken from a trance, Scally was called back to his own situation by the receptionist: "Substance abuse, alcoholism, or sex addiction?"

Scally thought for a moment, then his eyes went back to the

end of the hall where the Asian women had just been seconds ago.

* * * * *

Flopping down on the curb, Joey shoved a greasy slice from the neighborhood's finest pizzeria, Lenny & John's, into his mouth. As sauce threatened to make a run for his Adidas tracksuit, he tucked a napkin in the front of his jacket and smiled at the memories the fire wall inspired. This particular tracksuit had been Joey's favorite for several decades. And it showed.

A group of kids took notice as they dribbled a basketball past the curbside Brooklyn feast. "Hey, grandpa: nice Adidas look," shouted one. "Is that from 1980?" The quip was met with mocking laughter from the others.

Joey pulled what was left of his nearly devoured slice from his mouth. "Smart ass! As a matter of fact, it's from 1988. I bought it special for WrestleMania IV."

Another kid scoffed. "God, did they even have TVs then?"

Joey stood up. "I didn't watch it on TV! I was there!"

Showing off his own brand of humor, yet another kid put his hands on the side of his face in mocked surprise. "He was there!"

"He should frame those pants," the kid with the basketball chimed in.

"Yeah, whatta loser," the last kid spat as he grabbed the ball. He then took off as the rest of the group laughed and chased.

Joey looked down at his tracksuit. "Damn... can't even rock the Adidas anymore." Feeling defeated, he plopped back down on the curb.

Suddenly a great, bright light shined upon him, and Joey

WRESTLING WITH JOEYLICIOUS

turned to see a majestic figure standing where the annoying kids had just been. The man's hair was more like a rich, golden mane, and his skin glowed like he was a Greed god. Unlike Joey's pitiful apparel, the fantastic being wore a $10,000 suit. His eyes moved over the struggling wrestler, as if to size the mere mortal up. "Joseph Michael Cassata, a.k.a. Joeylicious?" he announced.

Feeling as if this was a dream, Joey squinted at the figure's glow before shielding his eyes. "God?"

His question was met with a proclamation: "It's time you were taught how to style and profile!"

As his eyes adjusted to the sun behind the man, Joey finally saw who it was addressing him. His jaw dropped. "The Nature Boy, Ric Flair! Even better!" He got on his knees, and bowed to the 16-time World Heavyweight Champion.

"Get up, Liscious. Someone might get the wrong idea."

Suddenly full of pep, Joey sprung to his feet.

"Let's go to work," Ric Flair continued.

Excitement coursed through Joey's entire being as he followed one of his mentors with glee. "You're gonna train me to be the Fifth Horseman?"

"No, I'm taking you for new threads. You wanna be the man, you gotta dress like the man."

"Wow, that sounds sick, but I just bounced a check getting my highlights done. I'm cleaned out til next month."

Ric waved a calm hand. "Don't worry, Lisch. It's all on the Nature Boy."

* * * * *

Feeling proud of his first step, Scally found himself "baring his soul" to a room full of sex addicts while he ate a chocolate donut. It didn't matter that Scally had only had sex once so far in his not so short life; this was progress! Although, did he actually have sex with Lisa Abromowitz that fateful autumn night in the 10th grade at Richie Guilio's house party? He was hammered as usual, and couldn't remember a damn thing. Lisa couldn't remember much either. After the supposed deed was done in the laundry room, she pretended to not even know who Scally was. They had four classes together that year, so this last detail was a bit suspect. Nonetheless, Scally was currently "baring" and the two Asian women that he followed in were eating it up. "I don't know what it is. I just can't stop havin' sex. I mean, over and over, day after day, night after night - I'm like a machine. And as soon as I'm done, I can start right up again."

Out of the corner of his eye, the little schemer noticed the two women sharing a look before leaning forward. They were clearly hooked. Now all Scally needed to do was reel them in. "Some lab should study me. I bet they'd come up with a formula for a new, super-Viagra."

The two women swooned, barely able contain themselves. Meanwhile, Scally could barely contain his smile. He had a thing for Asian women ever since he saw that hottie co-star with Christian Slater in the 1989 cult classic Gleaming the Cube. And now he actually had a chance to get his own cube gleamed - twice!

The sex addiction counselor cleared his throat. His expression was the exact opposite of Scally's. "Alright, Scally, thank you for sharing that. Again."

"Anytime," Scally beamed. "I'm here to start the healin'." His gaze shifted to the two women. "Maybe even spread it around if I can." This got a giggle out of the ladies.

"Well, I'll see some of you again tomorrow. Others...," the counselor looked directly at Scally, "...feel free to take the rest of the week off."

As the sex addiction session concluded, Scally stopped by the refreshment table for another donut or three. He wanted to take a little something with him, but he also wanted to give the two Asian beauties a chance to approach him.

Like moths drawn to a flame, they did just that. "Hi, Scally," the taller one said, speaking first.

Pretending to be surprised, the blonde deviant looked up from his donuts. "Oh, hey! It's Washi, isn't it?"

She nodded, then motioned to her friend. "And this is Sayo. Are you still up for spreading that healing?"

One of the donuts was halfway to Scally's mouth when he heard Washi's words. The donut stayed halfway to his mouth.

Sayo seemed a bit more nervous than her aggressive playmate. "We can go to your place," she suggested hesitantly, while softly touching Scally's puny arm.

Scally put the donuts down. All of them. "Is every meeting like this?"

Washi looked at her friend with uncertainty before turning back to Scally. "Is there a problem?"

His head shook vigorously. "No, no! What time is it?"

She looked over to the clock on the wall. "Almost three."

Scally's mind frantically went through the schedules of Joey and Mrs. Cassata before realizing that he couldn't possibly have planned this better. "Umm... perfect! My roommate should be out training."

The mere mention of someone else possibly joining the party excited Sayo even more. "Roommate?!"

Her friend was just as interested. "Training?"

With memories of what had happened (didn't happen) with all of his other potential female suitors over the decades, Scally made it abundantly clear that he was not offering Joey. "I mean, he's definitely not home," he clarified. Trying to erase the thought of another man cramping his style - especially Joey - he then motioned for the ladies to follow him. "C'mon."

Chapter 10
The Fifth Horseman

Ric Flair led Joey to the front of a high-end clothing store that the underdressed Italian would never have approached on his own. "Here we are," the wrestling legend announced, while holding out his arms.

Shaking his head, Joey did not feel comfortable. "But Naitch, I don't wear dress suits. I'm more of a tracksuit kind'a guy." To emphasize this, he pointed to the attire that the kids had just ridiculed him for attiring in.

His new mentor just gave him a knowing look. "Trust me on this."

Ric opened the door and ushered Joey inside. They were barely in the door when a snobby, bald-headed salesman was upon them. It must have been a slow day. Things were about to pick up.

"May I help you?" the salesman asked, forcing smile.

Joey watched as Ric took charge. "My prodigy will take two of your most expensive suits."

"Great! And when will your prodigy be arriving?"

Ric frowned and nodded toward Joey. "He's standing right next to me."

Bursting with pride, Joey puffed out his chest. The salesman quickly deflated such feelings. "Oh, I thought he was from the moving company."

Joey's forehead wrinkled. "You guys are moving?"

WRESTLING WITH JOEYLICIOUS

"No, you just look the part."

"And that's why we're here," Ric said, ending that confusion pointedly.

"Okay, then. Our most expensive suits go for about $7,500." The salesman was happy to get this so-called prodigy dressed and out the door before any of the store's more worldly patrons showed up.

The Nature Boy scoffed. "That's a little on the low end, but it'll have to do."

Joey reached out to stop Ric as he stepped forward. "Wait! What? Seven times- That's about..." His eyes seemed like they would roll to the back of his skull as he did the math. "That's almost 10 grand!"

"Nice try," Ric said with a smirk. "Good thing for you I have more money than Jesus."

This discombobulated Joey even more. "JC had bank? I thought the Sermon on the Mount was on the arm."

Ric looked at the putz incredulously.

"You know, the loaves and the fishes," Joey started to explain, feeling a bit foolish. "He actually paid for all that?"

Ric, as if this pointless talk of sermons and fishes was beneath him, just turned back to the salesman. "Bring him one in tan and one in black."

The salesman nodded and went to work, returning with a tan suit first.

Joey was ushered into the fitting room where he tried on a pair of pants. When he stepped out, he was given a shirt and tie. Finally, after the salesman put the tan jacket over Joey's inexperienced shoulders, the transformation was complete. The Italian Dream couldn't believe his eyes. He hadn't looked this good since Uncle Benny's funeral. Benny wasn't really Joey's uncle. He was just a guy from the neighborhood who everyone called Uncle Benny. In actuality, Benny was never anyone's Uncle; he was an only child. Poor Benny.

But lucky Joey! Behind him, Ric let out his trademark shout: "Woooooo, now we're talking! You could be one of the Horsemen dressed like that!"

"Wow! Really? You'll saddle me up?!" Joey could almost faint.

"Perhaps. But it's not just about the look. You also have to walk the walk."

Joey posed in front of a full-length mirror as he considered this business of walking the walk.

"Try it, Lisch," Ric called out.

"Like this?" A little off balance at first, Joey attempted the famous "Flair strut." It was not a pretty sight, and he completely lost confidence seeing how he looked in the mirror doing it.

"You look like a one-legged duck in heat. Here: try this on for size!" Ric was about to unleash the Nature Boy.

He grabbed a suit jacket off the rack, and threw it on the floor. An elbow drop to the sleeve quickly followed. And as the 16-time World Champ continued to beat on the jacket, Ric repeated over and over again at the top of his lungs: "WOOOOOOO! WOOOOOOO!"

Wanting nothing less than to emulate his hero, Joey grabbed another jacket off the rack and followed Ric's example. In between elbow drops of his own, he continued to practice the duck strut as he screamed "WOOOOOOOO" throughout the store.

"No, please! You're destroying them," the frantic salesman screamed. Too afraid to put his body on the line to stop the mayhem, he rushed away for help.

Ric and Joey continued their wrestling moves against the

helpless suites, throwing them all over the store and dropping elbows and knees on them. Successful blows were followed with frequent "woos" and strutting.

The destruction continued unabated for some time, until the salesman returned with the police behind him. "Arrest this lunatic," he cried, pointing at Joey.

Joey only became aware of his new surroundings when the cops grabbed him and slapped on the cuffs. Stunned, he looked at the manacles and then frantically scanned the store for Ric. "Wait! Whattaya doing? Naitch is gonna pay for everything!"

The cops looked around for Joey's accomplice, but Ric Flair was nowhere to be found. In fact, the Nature Boy was never actually there. It was becoming more and more apparent (or just plain apparent) that Joey had much bigger issues to deal with other than his under .500 wrestling record. He was Nucking Futs!

"He's been talking to himself since he came in," the salesman said to the cops, putting their minds at ease about the so-called accomplice. "Take him away! He's frightening the customers," he continued.

The other patrons were still crouched behind clothing racks uncertain that the flying carnage had ceased.

"And, yes, I am pressing charges for the damages," the salesman concluded, pointing at Joey.

"Hold on, I'll write you a check," Joey pleaded as the cops began to haul him toward the door. Desperate for help, he looked around for his tag team partner. "Ric? Naitch? Where are you?.. I'm still gonna be a Horseman, right?"

Chapter 11

Rapid Firing Sex Machine

Scally ushered Washi and Sayo into Joey's room. He nearly bumped into them as they looked around in awe. They were a mixture of intrigued and horrified. With all the wrestling posters, wrestling dolls, and fake championship belts hanging about, it was as if they had been lured into the den of a child or a serial killer. Or both.

Washi frowned. "What's all this?"

"My roommate's a collector," Scally responded, quick to dismiss what he was quite used to.

She looked at him with suspicion. "You share a bedroom?"

"Of course. We're roommates."

Sayo picked up a Jimmy "Superfly" Snuka doll. Unlike Washi, the charm of the paraphernalia suddenly grew on her. "Oh, how cute!"

Wanting to make the most of Sayo's more excepting feelings, Scally approached. "That's a specialty item."

Still not impressed with the decor, Washi decided it was time to get down to business. "Enough with the chatter," she said, sashaying over to Scally.

Sayo grinned in agreement. "It's about time we saw your specialty."

Things had never gone this smoothly for Scally in this department. And he was dead sober. He didn't have a clue on how to proceed. Gulping, he looked between the two beauties as they closed in on him from both sides.

* * * * *

Mrs. Cassata entered the apartment with groceries, and placed them on the kitchen counter. Peculiar sounds caught her attention. "Joey? You're home?" she called out, realizing they were coming from her son's bedroom.

There was no answer. Certain that she had heard something, Mrs. Cassata skipped putting away the groceries and headed straight for the room. She was halfway there when she remembered that another problem man-child lived with her rent free. Suddenly the noises, that were getting louder now, made more sense. "Oh," she muttered to herself, her tone more disappointment than relief. She almost wished it had been a burglar instead of Scally.

Still, she had given the bombastic blonde one last chance. Figuring she may as well see how that went, Mrs. Cassata opened the door. "Robert, how was your meet-" Her sentence was stabbed in the back as her eyes took in the unfathomable scene before her.

Scally, Washi, and Sayo were crammed into one bed fighting for space under Joey's "Italian Dream" sheets. It was clear nothing had really happened yet. The look of sexual frustration on the ladies' faces said it all.

Mrs. Cassata's initial shock quickly turned to rage. "What the hell is this?!"

Scally froze. "Mrs. C! You're early!"

Sayo took in the presence of Mrs. Cassata before turning back to Scally. "She's your mom?"

Washi shook her head. "He called her Mrs."

"My roommate's mom," Scally clarified.

WRESTLING WITH JOEYLICIOUS

Mrs. Cassata was the woman he should have clarified things with. She was just getting started. "This is what goes on when I'm not around?!"

Scally realized his mistake. "Nothing went on yet!" Of course, his reassurance was short lived. "But if you give me five minutes-"

Washi was more taken aback by his admission than from Mrs. Cassata's intrusion. "Five minutes?! You said you were a machine!"

"Yeah, a rapid firing machine," Scally responded casually, trying to placate the angry Asian.

"I'll give you five minutes," Mrs. Cassata screamed. There was no other warning as the fleet-footed sixty-five-year-old charged into the fray. Washi and Sayo leapt from the oncoming fury in their underwear, and scampered away from the bed.

Abandoned by his could've been but never was (as usual) playmates, Scally hid under the sheets.

With no lethal weapons available, Mrs. Cassata grabbed the nearest pillow and began pummeling her idiot son's idiot friend.

"Take it easy," Scally pleaded hopelessly. "I just started my healin'!"

Taking their cue from Mrs. Cassata, Washi and Sayo grabbed pillows of their own and joined in on the beat down. With nowhere to go and no way to retaliate, Scally just curled up into a ball and prayed for a quick death.

* * * * *

A few hours later, in the lobby of a police station, Scally sat slumped and defeated on a hard plastic chair. The bruises on his face and his matted hair made it clear that his beating did not end quickly. But he wasn't at the police station for his own indiscretions this time; his partner in crime had also been up to no good.

And this is what really threw Scally for a loop. In the past, he was always the one responsible for Joey's arrests. Like when they stole the statue of Saint Peter from one church and brought it to the garden of Saint Paul's Church; that was his idea, not Joey's. All Scally wanted to do was to show a biblical example of robbing Peter to pay Paul. But the churches and cops didn't respond well to the lesson.

Mrs. Cassata emerged from the interrogation room with Joey in tow. Her son was carrying the roughed up, tan and black suits from the store.

Seeing a ray of sunlight, Scally perked up. "Lisch, you made bail?"

Mrs. Cassata glared at her other useless mouth to feed. "We made an arrangement."

Scally looked his friend over. "What's with the suits?"

"I bought 'em on layaway. That's the arrangement." After answering the question, Joey finally took notice of his disheveled friend. "What happened to you?"

Before Scally could respond, Mrs. Cassata stopped the conversation cold. "Don't get me started on him."

Scally was beside himself. "You already got started!" Turning to his best friend, he pointed at the true culprit of his current misery. "Lisch, she burned your 'Italian Dream' sheets!"

"What?! Why?!"

Mrs. Cassata couldn't believe that she actually had to explain herself. "They were soiled in sin!"

"That was my last set," Joey cried, feeling betrayed. He

immediately directed his anger at the person whom he knew was truly at fault. "Scally, what the heck did you do?!"

"Me?!"

Not about to stand around listening to whining, Mrs. Cassata issued an order: "Let's go! Both of you! This isn't the place to advertise family business."

Leaving them no room to argue, she grabbed both knuckleheads by their shirt collars and dragged them toward the exit. "And you're both confessing to Father Randazzo this week!"

Chapter 12
Three's a Confessional Crowd

It was closing time at Rite Aid, and Joey hid off to the side just outside the store. He held a bouquet of flowers, and wore his tan suit which had a rather significant tear that ran down the back of the jacket. A bundle of nerves, he continuously adjusted his compromised outfit as he waited impatiently. Joey had really upset his mother this time, so he was going to do whatever he could to make it up to her. In the process, he hoped to find a little happiness of his own. The lights in the Rite Aid shut off, and Anne-Marie soon exited.

The instant she turned away to lock up, Joey popped up behind her. "Anne-Marie!"

She jumped, and dropped the keys at the unexpected and somewhat frightening call. "Jesus, Joey, you scared me," she shouted after quickly spinning back.

Looking apologetic, Joey retreated a step. "Oh, I'm sorry. Are you closing up? I just came to buy a vase for these flowers." He held up the bouquet.

Anne-Marie looked at them puzzled at first. "Uh... we don't sell vases."

Joey handed her the flowers.

Anne-Marie finally got the message, and was touched. To a point. "Thank you. They're beautiful." She finished locking up. "But I have to get home now, so-"

Joey wasn't willing to let her escape so soon. "Do you like

my suit?" he asked with a touch of desperation. "I just came from a big match, had to deal with the press..."

Anne-Marie looked at her old flame more closely. The flashy suit didn't fit the impression she was left with from their last encounter. "Dressed like that, you must be a success." Then again, she couldn't see the tear in the jacket from where she was standing.

"Yeah, I'm doing well," Joey beamed. "As a matter of fact, I have another match tomorrow night. You should come."

"Where at?" Anne-Marie asked hesitantly.

"Good Shepherd."

This seemed to confirm her suspicions. "The church?"

"The gym next to the church." Joey realized that he stepped in it, and quickly tried to recover. "I like to give back to the neighborhood when I can," he explained further.

Not entirely convinced, she again looked him up and down. "Oh... Well, that's good of you."

"So you'll come?"

"I'm not sure. I have a little girl now. It's tough to find a baby sitter on such short-" Suddenly, Anne-Marie couldn't complete her sentence. With her voice caught in her throat, she placed a hand over her mouth. She was upset.

Joey moved closer. "What's wrong?"

"We had a tragedy recently. My husband-"

Joey already knew where this was going. "He died?" he said, supplying the rest of the story. Trying to comfort his ex, he then reached out and hugged her.

Anne-Marie was clearly not expecting his response, and stood stiffly as Joey patted her back.

"That's terrible! And for it to happen so suddenly," Joey continued with his "comforting."

But Anne-Marie was no dummy. She could feel Joey's

forced sincerity with every forced pat, and pushed him away. "How did you know it was sudden?"

Now Joey had really stepped in it, and he immediately backpedaled. "You know... the accident. It must've been a shock."

Anne-Marie narrowed her eyes. "You knew this whole time, didn't you? Even when you came by last week."

This was definitely not the same girl who shared her Sno Balls with Joey, but he still tried to play dumb. "Whattaya mean?"

"Is that what this is? You see an opening 30 years later, and just show up as a shoulder to cry on?"

"No, no-" Joey frantically searched for a proper explanation. The search did not end well.

"I should get going." Anne-Marie abruptly brushed past him.

"Anne-Marie, wait," Joey called out, pulling out his last card to play. "I'm ready to settle down!"

She didn't even slow her fleeing strides.

As impossible as it was to believe, the second reunion between Joey and Anne-Marie outside Rite Aid was even worse than their first reunion inside.

* * * * *

Father Randazzo sat in the confessional booth adjusting his robes as he waited for the next sinner. It had already been a long session, and the good priest was dying to get out of there. TV Land's Murder She Wrote marathon was about to begin, and, by God, he was not going to miss a single rerun. Praying that his next confessor would be his last, he looked up as someone's hand pulled the screen shut from the other side of the booth. This would be a secret confession. At least that's what it was intended to be.

"Bless us Father for we have sinned?"

Fr. Randazzo knew the voice as soon as Joey opened his mouth. He was about to respond normally, but one of the words in that sentence struck him as an oddity. "Us?"

"Yeah, there's two of us." Scally's voice was also unmistakable.

He didn't need the verification, but the priest couldn't help but ask: "Robert, is that you?"

"I thought he couldn't see us," the blonde tornado said, hissing at Joey.

The priest thought he heard someone get smacked in the head.

"He can't," Joey responded harshly.

Of course, that was Scally's head.

Fr. Randazzo tried his best to remain calm. "Joseph, what are you two up to?" he asked hesitantly. Murder She Wrote was definitely going to have to wait. The priest could almost kick himself for not DVRing it.

"Well, it's like this Father: you're our priest, but you're also our employer."

"Your employer," Scally corrected.

"Right, he fired your ass."

"Joseph, please," Fr. Randazzo shouted, quickly cutting off that kind of talk.

Then, quite surprisingly, the priest heard uncertainty in his young (still employed) gym teacher's voice: "Whatever I say in here, can't be used against me at work, right? You know, like attorney/client privilege."

"So that means he can use things against me?! Why am I even here?" Scally's input was as asinine as the priest could have expected.

"Why do I have a feeling both of you will be reciting the entire rosary after this?" Fr. Randazzo asked as much as stated. Par for the course, he was struggling with his role with these two.

"There's no time for that, Father." Joey was quick to prevent the priest from administrating his usual penance. "We're on our way to a match."

"Go ahead," the priest sighed. Anything to get this chore over with for Angela Lansbury's sake at least.

Unfortunately, those two tiny, and on the surface, harmless words opened up a floodgate of sins that Fr. Randazzo had no chance of stemming. He couldn't differentiate between Joey's transgressions and Scally's. But he could guess.

"One at a time! Jesus," the priest cried out, unable to control himself any longer.

There was a moment of silence from the other side of the booth. "Now, now, Father," Joey eventually said in the midst of reprimanding his own priest, "we wouldn't want someone else to have to confess while we're in here."

Chapter 13
Bingo & B.R.A.W.L.

There it was in not so bright letters on the not so impressive marque just outside the gymnasium of Good Shepherd's elementary school.

Joey, wearing his new black suit (minus the sleeves), stood with Una Grenada and Milk Shake as they glared up at the unflattering placement of their precious, albeit, unflattering wrestling league. It was Saturday night, and the boys should have been raring to go in their pre-fight attire. But, alas, on this Saturday night they were not.

"Why are we second banana?" Joey said, voicing his displeasure first.

Even though Una Grenada was equally displeased, he decided to play devil's advocate for the sake of Bingo. "I think it's alphabetical. 'B, I' – 'B, R'."

Joey shook his head, unwilling to accept that logic. "We have a dot after our 'B'."

"Do dots come before 'I'?" Milk Shake asked, sincerely curious.

"Of course, they do," Joey shot back.

Una Grenada cared less and less by the second. "We'll have to get a judge's ruling on that," he simply responded.

"The clock on the wall says it's time to BRAWL," an all too familiar voice called out from a distance. Scally materialized with a Styrofoam cup of beer firmly in hand. He was already drunk, and it wasn't even eight o'clock yet. Okay, it was five after.

Milk Shake looked about as annoyed as Joey felt. "Here comes your honor now." Scally may have been the lanky wrestler's arch nemesis outside the ring, but he would have loved to get his hands on him inside.

Joey folded his arms at his so-called manager. "Where the heck did you go?"

"Stopped by McFadden's. My credit's still good there." It was common knowledge that Scally had open tabs in every bar in the Brooklyn diocese. Apparently, McFadden's didn't get the memo.

"You just told Father Randazzo you started AA!" Joey couldn't believe the gall. Well, he could believe it, but still.

"Can't a man celebrate his sobriety?" Scally said, adjourning the argument. He downed the rest of his beer, and tossed the empty cup aside with no trash can in sight.

Una Grenada and Milk Shake just headed toward the gymnasium. Joey shook his head and did the same.

* * * * *

The setup inside the BRAWL venue was even more disappointing than the marque. There was no ring, and not a single wrestling material was to be found. Instead, there was just a bunch of senior citizens playing Bingo. Still. And a rough looking bunch of old timers at that: missing teeth, eye patches, even a few wooden legs. They looked like an elderly biker gang, minus the leather jackets and bikes. Joey and the boys looked around unable to comprehend what they were seeing. It was bad enough that Bingo had top billing over them, but they should have wrapped up their last game some time ago.

Scally burst through the wrestlers, and saw what made them stop dead in their tracks. "I know I'm lit, but did we step into another dimension."

Joey frowned. "They're supposed to be done and gone by 7:30."

Una Grenada pulled out his cell and glanced at the time. "It's after eight."

"And Tiny fights you in 10 minutes," Milk Shake added.

Joey held out his hands in utter frustration. "They don't even have the ring set up!"

Una Grenada noticed what the others didn't, and pointed across the facility. "Well, it looks like Lou's on it."

Sure enough, Lou Rossati was having a heated discussion with the Monsignor of Good Shepherd. And the Monsignor, also a senior, looked like a tough hombre in his own right.

Making the best of a bad situation, Scally headed to a Bingo table. "I'm gettin' in this mutha! There's money on the line!"

Joey ignored his manager's quick abandonment, and continued to gripe: "This is ridiculous! I busted out my new look and everything!"

Una Grenada took a good gander at the Italian Dream. "Yeah, that jacket's pretty badass. It came like that - without the sleeves?"

"Uh... not exactly," Joey answered with some embarrassment, briefly reflecting on the suit store fiasco.

Lou, finally spotting his wrestlers, headed their way. He was clearly just as pissed about what was going on. "C'mon, let's go! We're canceled here tonight!"

"Damn, man!" Milk Shake slumped and looked around. He had hoped they would salvage the evening somehow.

WRESTLING WITH JOEYLICIOUS

Joey wasn't willing to give up so easily. "Whattaya mean we're canceled?! We're the main event!"

Lou patted Joey on the arm in an effort to comfort the veteran wrestler. "We didn't sell enough tickets, and Bingo's running late."

"So we can start later! I haven't missed a Saturday night match in 20 years!" Joey wasn't kidding. He really hadn't. He even broke his arm once during a bizarre cannoli eating incident. That occurred on a Saturday afternoon at the Feast of San Gennaro, and Joey still wrestled that night - albeit in excruciating pain.

"Sorry, kid. But even Gehrig's streak came to an end," Lou said, having seen it all. This was just another miserable night in his mostly miserable existence.

One of the senior women turned and glared at the intrusion of wrestlers. "Keep it down back there," she spat, smacking her gums together. "I can't hear the numbers!"

Mockingly holding up his hands, Milk Shake tried to placate the old broad in an undiplomatic way. "Take it easy, grandma. Maybe turn up your listenin' device."

Her eyes glowed red. "Screw you, you... non-white person!"

"Oh, snap," Una Grenada coughed up, realizing he was also a non-white person.

One of the senior men sitting next to the old racist turned to voice his opinion of the BRAWL crew. He looked like a typical retired wiseguy straight from Martin Scorsese central casting. "Check out the getup on these guys! Looks like The Village People are back in town!"

This caused the rest of the seniors to join in on the verbal abuse party. "Where's the cop and the chief?" someone called out from the back.

This got a round of uproarious laughs, and the wrestlers were

WRESTLING WITH JOEYLICIOUS

reaching their breaking point.

Milk Shake cracked his knuckles. "I'm about to whoop some senior citizen ass," he muttered.

"Sign me up," Una Grenada added, seconding the motion.

Suddenly, Scally leapt up from the table he had planted himself at. "Bingo!"

The hag next to the drunken imposter stood up shakily. "That's my card!" She reached out trying to snatch it.

Scally quickly moved the card to his other hand and held it high. "Finders keepers, losers weepers!"

An old man with an eye patch stood up and grabbed the Bingo menace. "Give it back to her," he shouted, trying to pull the card from Scally's dancing hand.

Joey saw that his friend required parental intervention. Again. "I better get in there," he said to the other two wrestlers.

Scally screamed and gyrated as he desperately tried to keep his Bingo winner from the growing number of wrinkled and veiny hands working just as desperately to snag it. "Paws off! She can collect on the next round!"

Joey stepped into the fray, hoping to resolve things more peacefully. Seniors were a reasonable age demographic after all. "Scal, knock it off!" He tried to grab the Bingo card as well.

Suddenly, the focus of the senior citizens' rage turned toward Joey. "Who are you now?" the one with the eye patch asked incredulously.

"Nice jacket, ginzo," a sweet old lady with a pink sweater hollered from somewhere in the vicinity.

Taking umbrage, Joey's eyes darted around in search of the self-proclaimed fashion critic. "Who said that?!"

Meanwhile, several of the more ruthless Bingo players began to surround Una Grenada and Milk Shake. Up until that point the two wrestlers of color had stayed on the sidelines, but the Italian Dream knew that wouldn't last.

"Guys! Get outta there," Joey called out, waving at his BRAWL companions. "It's not worth it!"

Suddenly, a single and familiar, god-like voice rose above the clamor: "Woooooo!!!"

Joey looked to the distance, and saw Rick Flair mauling a group of seniors on the other side of the gym. "The Nature Boy," he called out, unable to believe his eyes at first.

Before the blonde Adonis was able to respond to his biggest fan, Ric was overrun by another gaggle of bloodthirsty old timers. It was time for Joeylicious to rescue his hero. "Don't worry, Naitch! The Fifth Horseman rides!"

As Joeylicious charged forward, an all-out brawl erupted. The wrestlers were severely outnumbered, but they had middle age on their side. Lou even got into the swing of things as he squared off against the Monsignor. Tables and chairs were turned over, Bingo cards flew through the air, and Scally's screams echoed throughout the venue as he got his ass kicked by a bunch of little old ladies.

Reaching Ric Flair, who was still in the midst of fighting valiantly, Joeylicious bellowed his hero's famous battle cry: "Woooooo!!!" Then he launched himself into the action, thus keeping his Saturday night wrestling streak alive and well. All of the tension, frustration, and aggression flowed from Joeylicious as he refused to turn down any white-haired foe willing to face him.

The brawl was in full swing, but something near the front of the gym caught Joeylicious's attention. As if in slow motion, he turned to see the last person he had expected to see that night.

Standing at the entrance was Anne-Marie, a look of shock

WRESTLING WITH JOEYLICIOUS

and horror on her face. Holding her hand was her four-year-old daughter and miniature twin, Veronica, who was more awed by the spectacle than shocked. It took a moment before Anne-Marie could actually believe what her eyes were seeing. And it took another moment before she realized that her daughter was seeing the same thing. She quickly pulled Veronica close to her and shielded her eyes.

Joeylicious's fists stopped flying. "Anne-Marie?" he said, practically breathing her name.

But before he could get a response from his one-time lover - not that a response was coming - a frail senior snuck up behind him. With a steel folding chair in hand, the diabolical old timer struck the Italian Dream over the head and put him to sleep. For real. The last thing Joey remembered before he fell to the floor unconscious was the memorable look on Anne-Marie's face. As impossible as it was to believe, their third reunion, was even worse than their first two. Combined.

Chapter 14

The Four Faces of Foley

Mrs. Cassata stood beside her son's hospital bed, any concern she may have felt was not obvious by her demeanor. What was clear was her annoyance at the situation. Joey looked like he had been the victim of an accident, just not a particularly gruesome one. The bandage around his head looked more like a precaution, as there was no visible blood seeping through. If there was blood, and lots of it, his mother may have been more sympathetic. After all, it was now Sunday morning, and she was forced to miss church over the previous night's fiasco. If Joey was going to interrupt her time with God, his injury should have at least been severe enough to land him on the doorstep of the pearly gates.

Sitting in a chair beside her nicked up man-child was the ever-present Scally. Although he didn't outwardly show it, he was a bit more concerned about the injury than she was. Not so much for Joey's overall health, but at the prospect of his Saturday night wrestling streak being put into jeopardy. Mauling a bunch of Bingo playing seniors saved Joey's streak this time, but would BRAWL allow him to wrestle in a sanctioned match with his head still wrapped in bandages? Those needed to come off, and quick. Unless there was another way. Scally's little mind mulled over the possibilities.

Mrs. Cassata rubbed her lips, thinking of a way to verbalize her feelings. "When the hell are you gonna give up this wrestling crap?" she finally spouted.

This was not quite the way Joey had expected the conversation to start. Given that he was laid up in the hospital, he had hoped that his own mother, at least, would show a little tenderness. His disappointment was obvious. "C'mon, Ma," he whined. "I just got hit with a chair a little awkwardly."

That was not even remotely close to what Mrs. Cassata wanted to hear. As if to emphasis the point, she smacked her son upside the head. Still no blood. This only made her angrier.

More startled than hurt, Joey put his hand on his bandages. "What was that for?" he cried.

His mother glared down at him. "Because you're over 40 and still getting hit by chairs!" She then reached out and swatted the boa around his neck, her blood pressure continuing to rise. "And why do you have to wear those stupid feathers in here?!"

"It's my signature look," Joey replied, pulling away a little.

"You never know when the paparazzi's gonna come around," Scally added, sticking up for his best friend.

Clearly pleased with that answer, Joey attempted to fist bump his grinning manager, but his arm couldn't quite complete the trip from his position in bed. They ended up more knuckle grazing than fist bumping, until they tried again. This time, with a lot more cheese to it, they properly bashed fists, and then beamed as if they had actually accomplished something of cultural merit. Mrs. Cassata could only shake her head in disgust.

Mercifully, the scene of motherly disappointment and displaced revelry was interrupted when an orderly stepped into the room carrying breakfast for the patient. As the orderly rested the tray in front of Joey, a small cartoon of milk on it seemed to shine like a neon sign. The orderly, paying little attention to this and not caring either way, just turned around and left without saying a word.

Joey was clearly upset as he held up the tiny milk. "Ma, they gave me one percent," he bemoaned. "You know this hurts my tummy!"

Mrs. Cassata's expression softened. They had finally reached a topic where she could feel some empathy for her child. One percent milk messed with her innards as well, and this situation would soon be rectified. "I know, my special boy," she said lovingly, patting Joey on the head. "Let me see what I can do."

Joey smiled as he watched her turn and leave, her motherly instincts finally kicking in. "Thanks, Ma. You're the best!"

A nurse popped her head in the room, and took a peek at Joey's chart. Her striking features immediately caught Scally's attention. Yes. She was Asian.

Scally gazed at her longingly. Was this his chance at redemption after his last journey to the Far East with Washi and Sayo crashed into the sea? When the nurse turned and left, Scally had a half grin on his face. "I think my yellow fever's actin' up. Time to renew my prescription."

Without waiting for or even needing his friend's acknowledgement or encouragement, Scally took off after the Asian goddess in scrubs. He would not be returning soon. Joey simply shook his head at Scally's political incorrectness before noticing that an extremely large male doctor was suddenly standing at the foot of his bed with his back facing him. Thinking that the doctor must have entered behind the nurse, Joey just waited patiently for whatever he had to say.

The sound of Scally's fleeting footsteps echoed through the hall when the doctor finally spoke. It was not at all what Joey had expected. "We're here to toughen you up, Lisch."

The doctor spun around and Joey's eyes widened as he

~ 94 ~

marveled at the WWE legend, Mick Foley.

"Mick Foley?! What are you doing here?"

"I'll address that momentarily. But first, let me state that it's great to be here... right here... in Brooklyn, New York!" The two-time world champion knew how to properly announce one's arrival.

His words were punctuated by a groan of pain from the other unseen patient in the room. Joey looked over at the room's divider curtain as Mick acknowledged the sound. "Thank you," he simply said.

Then the Micker was right back on topic. "But my main purpose for being here, Joey, is not to get a 'cheap pop' from the gentleman behind the curtain. It's to teach you how to become hard-core."

"Uh... I think I'm pretty hard-core already." Pointing at his bandaged head, Joey felt that this was all the evidence needed to show his commitment to the art of getting one's ass kicked.

Mick shook his head, and sneered. "You just sent your mother out to get you milk that doesn't give you a tummy ache."

"I'm lactose intolerance!"

Slamming his clipboard to the floor, Mick strode forward. "Then switch to soy or almond milk!"

This suggestion baffled the patient. "Almond milk? How do you make milk from almonds?"

Folding his arms across his chest, professor Mick began to explain in detail: "Actually, it's a very delicate process. As you know, Joey, almonds have no nipples."

The Italian head bandage nodded in agreement, the whole idea completely beyond his comprehension.

"So therefore it's necessary to grind them into a fine paste," Mick continued, "and then siphon off all the pulp. Very important."

"Is that like a 'Foley' family recipe?" Joey was really into this learning thing now. He was about to take notes.

Mick gave his student a quick punch to the face to dispel such notions. "That's enough about milk! Now man up, Licious and listen here! My former employer didn't see the potential in me until I was thrown off of a 27 foot tall steel structure. But after I was thrown off that 42 foot tall steel structure, I was world champion all because of a perilous 90 foot plunge!"

Feeling his excitement rise, Joey sat up straight. "You know what? You're right," he said, ignoring the new pain. "Watch this!" Grabbing the closest thing at hand, he slammed the one percent milk cartoon against his head causing it to explode all over him and Mick.

"That is not quite what I had in mind," Mick muttered, wiping the milk from his face. "Nurse," he suddenly called out. "We're going to need some help!"

Like magic, a male nurse wearing a hippie T-shirt, sunglasses and a tie-dye bandana appeared at the foot of Joey's bed. His surprise quickly turned to excitement as Joey realized he was looking at Mick Foley's alter ego, Dude Love.

"Ow, Doctor Foley," Dude Love said. "Is there a need for some naughty nursing?"

Joey grabbed his bed sheet, and wiped the milk from his eyes. This did not change what he saw. "No way! Dude Love?!"

The colorful male nurse smiled as he strutted to Joey's bedside opposite Mick, and held up his hand. "Up high, daddy!"

Joey excitedly stretched, and gave the friendly wrestler a high five.

WRESTLING WITH JOEYLICIOUS

Dude then lowered his hand with the palm facing up. "Down low!"

Joey grinned like a fool as he attempted a low five, but Dude pulled his hand away for the miss. "You're too slow."

Mick laughed. "He got ya! Don't worry about it, Joey. He get's all of us." He was very pleased as he pointed proudly at his alter ego. "Good one, Dude!"

Joey frowned as if he was suddenly putting things together. "Wait a second..." His eyes went back and forth between Mick and Dude Love. "Aren't you two the same per-"

Dude simply shook his head. "Daddy, the dude understands your plight. But understand that kickin' heavy duty booty was never exactly the dude's bag. All the dude was ever interested in was making sweet, sweet love. But then the Micker and his friends taught the dude about a different type of love: tough love!"

That brought further confusion to Joey. "Mick's friends? Who are you talking about?"

"No one knows more about tough love than these cooky cats!" Dude Love pulled back the divider curtain to reveal the other "patient" in the room.

To Joey's surprise, he had been sharing a room with Mick's other alter egos: hard-core legends Cactus Jack and Mankind. Cactus Jack strode forward holding a baseball bat wrapped in barbwire, and singing "Take Me Out to the Ball Game." Behind him, Mankind picked up a steel chair and followed with a wicked grin barely visible under his surgical mask.

Joey's eyes darted around the room in fear. "Uh, guys... not that I'm not super excited to meet you, but can we talk about this for a second?"

Mick Foley simply laughed at Joey's pathetic plea. "Go get em' boys!"

WRESTLING WITH JOEYLICIOUS

Mankind stepped around Cactus Jack and lifted the steel chair high, his ominous words muffled by the mask: "What goes up...," Joey watched helplessly as the chair crashed down on his already injured head, "...must come down!"

The pain was much worse than what he received from the old timer's blow at the Bingo brawl, and Joey would probably spend another night or two in the hospital for it.

Dude Love held up a hand. "Lighten up, Manny!"

Cactus Jack continued to sing as he wrapped the barbwire baseball bat around Joey's neck, choking him.

"Ow! There are barbs on that wire," Dude Love warned. The poor patient barely made out his words.

But through all the mayhem and pain, Joey could not, for the life of him, figure out how Mick Foley was doing all this. It was Mick and all three of his alter egos in the same room at the same time. Was it an optical illusion? Were they secretly quadruplets? Or was he (meaning Joey himself) just plain crazy? Although the third scenario was the obvious route to investigate, Joey still dwelled on the first two.

Interrupting Joey's inner deliberations, Mankind flung the chair to the side. "I'll take it from here, Cactus. You already made your point." A strange expression passed over his face as he considered his own words. "Point," he chuckled. "Good one, Dude!"

Without warning, he grabbed Joey, and launched him onto the other hospital bed. Then Mankind reached into his pants and pulled out his own alternate personality, Mr. Socko – a literal sock puppet - and placed it over his arm. Mr. Socko felt no need to introduce himself to Joey. "Have a pleasant afternoon," he announced instead, skipping right to the fond farewell.

Joey dreaded what was next. But his dread quickly turned to

WRESTLING WITH JOEYLICIOUS

disgust when Mr. Socko was shoved into his gapping mouth, which caused him to choke. "AHHHHHHHH!!!"

Cactus Jack stood on the side and laughed. "Bang, bang!"

Dude Love stood on the other side looking approvingly at the events unfolding. "Love can be very painful, daddy."

Suddenly, the Asian nurse rushed back into the room with "you know who" on her coattails. Once again Scally's prescription for his Asian persuasions was not renewed. In fact, it was never filled in the first place. He was obviously frustrated by this, but his demeanor quickly changed when he came face to face with the real disaster at hand.

"What the hell is going on in here?" the nurse demanded, well beyond concerned.

Joey was about to explain, but Mick Foley and his alter egos had all managed to escape without another word or trace. He looked down at what should have been Mr. Socko on Mankind's arm, but saw the foot of an elderly patient shoved inside his mouth instead.

The battered old timer was someone Joey vaguely recognized, but he certainly was not another version of Mick Foley - even if Mick had returned from a time machine some 25 years later. Instead, it was the disgruntled Bingo player who hit Joey with the chair that sent him to the hospital in the first place. "Get this maniac off of me," the pained senior bellowed.

He pulled his foot out of Joey's mouth, but the frantic Italian wasn't ready to let someone's fragile grandfather off the hook that easily. It was difficult to accept that Mick Foley and his alter egos had managed to get away, so Joey continued to wrestle with the elderly patient's leg almost in protest.

Clearly worried about his safety, the patient looked accusingly at the nurse. "He slammed his milk against his head, and started screaming about being hard-core!"

WRESTLING WITH JOEYLICIOUS

It was at that moment that a beaming Mrs. Cassata returned with her son's lactose free milk. "Look what momma got for-" The smile froze on her face as she took in the scene.

Joey immediately sought her help with more pressing issues: "Ma, help me! Mick and his friends are beating me up!"

The elderly patient grabbed a nearby bedpan and struck Joey over the head with it, knocking him unconscious. "I'm not even Irish, you racist bastard," the old man hollered. "Stop calling me Mick!"

It suddenly dawned on Scally that this was the same senior who had knocked Joey out the previous night. "Again?!"

Mrs. Cassata was like a statue as she stared at the aftermath. Her son, in the midst of some kind of mid life crisis, finally had blood seeping through his bandaged head. It was quite apparent that the afternoon mass at church would be missed as well.

Chapter 15

The Intervention

Double-parked in front of the hospital with the engine already running, Mrs. Cassata sat behind the wheel of her 2007 Honda Civic with Scally at her side. Joey had just exited the hospital in a wheelchair, and was now being pushed toward them by the same orderly who brought him the infamous one percent milk.

The orderly hit the brakes just outside the hospital doors. "Okay, time to get off."

Joey looked up at him incredulously. "The car's like 15 feet away!"

Scally, having no patience to begin with, leaned over the console between the two front seats of the Honda and blasted the horn three times. Mrs. Cassata gave him a look of displeasure, which he, of course, didn't notice. "C'mon, Joe! Real Housewives of Atlanta starts in 20 minutes," he called out, as if the horn weren't enough to motivate his friend's expediency.

Joey waited expectantly for the orderly to keep pushing. He could've waited a week. It didn't matter. The orderly was clocking out. "I'm sure you can walk from here."

Finally, Joey pushed himself out of the wheelchair in a huff. "I gotta do something about my insurance," he grumbled.

Witnessing the dramatic turn of events, Scally leaned out the window. "Hop in, Lisch! Road to recovery, baby!"

WRESTLING WITH JOEYLICIOUS

Joey stopped just outside the passenger door. "It's my mom's car. You sit in the back." This was obvious protocol for children of any size. If someone's parent was driving, their friend forfeited access to the car radio.

Scally surrendered with a sigh. Too lazy to get out of the car and walk a full step, he haphazardly climbed over the seat and accidentally kicked Mrs. Cassata in the head before settling in the back. He was entirely unaware of his transgression. What else is new?

Mrs. Cassata ignored Scally's clumsiness. A kick to the head was a fair price to pay if the alternative was him sitting next to her. She had her son to deal with and that was quite enough. "All set, your highness?"

Joey sniffed like a little boy who had been pouting before opening the passenger side door and climbing in. He knew that another chewing out was coming, but he prayed for silence at least for a little while. The tension in the car was palpable as Mrs. Cassata pulled away and drove them home.

* * * * *

Joey and Scally sat on the living room couch of the Cassata apartment watching Real Housewives of Atlanta with a giant bowl of popcorn between them. Scally was hogging the buttery snack as usual, but Joey didn't mind. He was enjoying their favorite TV show, and his mother had not broken up the party. Yet. This last detail gnawed at him. As much as he was enthralled with the trials and tribulations of Debbie and her husband in Atlanta, Joey knew it was only a matter of time before his mother put her final stamp on the disastrous weekend. She actually missed Sunday mass. And her streak of going to church every Sunday was even longer than his

WRESTLING WITH JOEYLICIOUS

Saturday night wrestling one. Of course, this was all his fault and Joey knew he would hear about it before the lights went out.

As if reading her son's mind, Mrs. Cassata entered from the kitchen and, without a word, turned off the TV.

Scally sat up in protest. "Hey!"

"C'mon, Ma! Debbie's husband just canceled her shopping credit card," Joey added, doing his best to play dumb.

The expression on Mrs. Cassata's face said it all. She didn't give a damn about Debbie, her husband or her credit cards. She only had one thing on her mind. "We need to talk."

It was time to take his medicine, and Joey knew it. He sat back. "Alright, so talk."

Her eyes drifted to Scally. "Are you sure you want your friend to hear this?"

"Scally and I have no secrets." The honest truth was Joey thought his mother would hold back the real hellfire if the blonde imp was at his side. Scally might even chime in with something dumb enough to deflect her anger. Yes, that part would absolutely happen.

Feeling proud of his client's endorsement, Scally sat on the edge of the couch. "Yeah, Mrs. C. You know that."

Mrs. Cassata wiped her hand across her mouth as she sat down. She was clearly searching for the right words. "It's happening again." There was no anger in her tone.

Joey, relieved by her tone at least, just waited patiently for his mother to elaborate. "What is?" he finally asked when she didn't say anything else.

She gritted her teeth. "You know what. You're seeing your imaginary wrestling friends again."

Waving a hand, he dismissed her concern. "That was nothing. I took a blow to the head."

WRESTLING WITH JOEYLICIOUS

Scally's eyes shifted to Joey. It was a subject he was hoping to let slide, but now that Mrs. Cassata had brought it up, he knew that he needed to say his peace as well. The expression on his face let Joey know that even his best friend and manager wasn't buying his bull.

"What?" Joey asked, again playing dumb.

Scally looked away. "I think I witnessed a few episodes myself - even before the injury." This was more than true. Even putting the Bingo incident with imaginary Ric Flair aside, Scally had recently found Joey rolling around on his bedroom floor with a "Rowdy" Roddy Piper doll that he was convinced was the real McCoy. This was particularly strange because the great Piper had unfortunately passed away some time ago, so was Joey now seeing ghosts as well?

Mrs. Cassata's face was unusually expressive, and it radiated concern. "Sweetie, when this was happening when you were a kid, it was cute. But you're over 40 now. Maybe you should see someone."

Scally hesitated for a moment. "Are you seein' anyone now?"

Joey gave his friend a strange look, as if Scally should already know that he hadn't been talking to a shrink.

"No, I mean in this room with us?" the blonde inquisitor added, realizing he needed to provide clarification.

Joey's eyes drifted to a manic figure suddenly standing behind his mother. It was Mankind waving his arms. "Say no! Say no!"

Joey couldn't pull his eyes away from the crazed wrestler, let alone find his voice to respond to Scally's question.

"Otherwise, they'll put you away like they did to me," Mankind shouted, continuing to warn him.

Mrs. Cassata frowned, thinking that her son was resenting

~ 104 ~

her inquiries and glaring at her instead. "Don't look at me like that."

Scally patted his friend's arm. "Hey, I'm gettin' help for my problem."

That was all it took to get Joey to snap out of it. Turning an angry look to his scheming pal, there was a lot Joey wanted to say. He knew very well that Scally wasn't getting help, and whatever he was getting was only making things worse.

"Don't look at him like that either," his mother said, pulling his attention back to her. "Robert's making an effort."

"Yeah," Scally beamed.

Petulantly, Joey sat back on the couch. Clearly they were ganging up on him. "I'm not crazy, okay?"

Knowing that her son wasn't going to listen to reason, Mrs. Cassata figured she would put her foot down where she felt she could. "Well, you're at least listening to your physical doctor, and taking a break from wrestling. For a while!"

Joey was flabbergasted. "What about my streak?!"

Mrs. Cassata stood up and glared down at her son. "I don't care! You had a concussion! One more hit to the head, and who knows?"

Scally nodded in agreement. "Yeah, Lisch. You're already seein' stars."

Joey shoved Scally off the couch and halfway across the room.

His mother put her hands on her hips. "Joey!"

Joey looked down at his friend with satisfaction. "Who's seeing stars now?" he gloated.

Chapter 16
Small Helmet, Smaller Office

After barely convincing his mother that he needed to at least continue his exercise regime while mending, Joey made his way to Marine Park. It didn't bother him one bit that he was over 40, and still needed his mother's permission for such things. Living rent free had its price. Dressed in sweats, he pulled out a jump rope at the concrete area next to the jogging path and began to stretch with it. Scally ambled over with a batting helmet tucked under his arm.

"Here, put this on," Scally said, his managerial skills quickly on display.

Joey looked down at the hard plastic object. "Why?"

"Why do ya think? To protect your head."

"I'm about to jump rope."

"You're workin' out. Anybody can get hurt durin' a workout." Did Scally really need to state the obvious?

As ridiculous as he felt about it, Joey was in no mood to argue. Snatching the helmet, he attempted to put it on his head. Nothing doing. It was way too tight, and it wouldn't even get past his ears. Joey continued to struggle with it anyway. "What size is this?"

"I don't know. It fit me at the store." Scally obviously didn't take into account certain mathematical elements. The helmet fit Joey's head in the same way The Haiti Kid's tights would fit Andre The Giant.

WRESTLING WITH JOEYLICIOUS

"Your head's the size of a peanut!" Joey was actually in pain now. He was about to be in agony.

Unwilling to give up before exhausting all options, Scally had a brilliant idea. "Hang on!" Without warning, he jumped up as high as he could and slammed down on the helmet with both of his open palms. If this sounded like an earthquake inside Joey's head, it felt a whole lot worse. But the helmet did manage to make its way past his ears before crashing down on his skull.

Joey pulled away. "Ow! Watch it! I'm coming off a concussion!"

"I know. That's why I brought the helmet." Well, who could argue with that?

Joey pinched his fingers in front of Scally's face. "I'm this close to pile driving you through concrete."

Scally waved his friend's hand away, and scoffed. "Let's go. Focus. Only a few days til your next match." He stepped back as his one and only client began to jump rope.

This proved to be a much harder task than usual for Joey with the extra inches of helmet in the way. The rope kept striking the plastic appendage, throwing off his rhythm. He halted his workout in frustration. "I can't jump rope with this thing on! It's too big."

"You just said it was too small," Scally countered, not following that logic.

Joey's glare was far less effective through the helmet. "I mean, high."

"How can it be high and small at the same time?"

"It's higher than where my head usually is, okay?!" That settled the clarification. Or did it? Fed up either way, Joey tried to pull the helmet off. Not a chance. "Great! Now it's stuck!"

Scally rolled his eyes. "Let me see that." He tugged on the

helmet with all his puny might, but his friend quickly pushed him away.

"Stay away from me!" Joey went back to work on the helmet himself, but his efforts proved to be even more futile. Suddenly, he gave up all together. "Quick! Hide this!" He threw the jump rope at his manager in a panic.

Baffled, Scally looked around and spotted a female jogger heading in their general direction. "Hey, isn't that Anne-Marie?"

"She can't see the jump rope," Joey hissed. "Her husband died using that!"

"Of a head injury," Scally mused, seeing his friend's point. "And you're wearin' a helmet."

"Exactly! Get rid of it!"

Instead, Scally took the opportunity to yank on the helmet again.

"The rope," Joey wailed, pushing him away again. "Get rid of the rope!"

But it was too late. Anne-Marie had pretty much reached them, and she started to slow realizing who and what her eyes were adjusting to.

Joey gave her a quick wave. "Hi, Anne-Marie! Nice day, huh?" he spat out with forced pleasantry. "I see we're both getting in a workout."

Trying to rectify the situation, Scally held up the rope. "But he's totally not jump-roping! I am! He just happens to be wearin' a helmet for protection." The idiot shook the rope as if the emphasis would convince her.

Joey awkwardly laughed that off as Anne-Marie gave them a confused look. Without a word, she jogged right on past them - even picking up her pace to a near sprint.

Joey watched in humiliation as her silhouette quickly

disappeared down the jogging path, which was now a running path. As soon as she was out of sight, he shoved his little troublemaker once more. "Scally, you idiot!"

*****

Lou sat at his cluttered desk in his equally cluttered and cramped office. To say this was not the ideal place for a meeting with a group of wrestlers, would have been the understatement of the century. A few skinny dwarves would've had trouble squeezing into this rat hole with Lou and his desk, never mind three members of BRAWL and one unqualified manager. Taking in his boys, Lou's eyes stopped on Joey who was wearing a baseball helmet. Uncertain what to say about that, his gaze continued over to Scally, Una Grenada and Milk Shake. Understandably, they were all jostling for elbow room.

With a sigh, Lou decided to get things started. "Alright, guys. You probably know why I called this meeting tonight-"

"Where's Shamrock?" Joey immediately asked. "He don't have to show?"

Lou waved away his concern. "Don't worry about Shamrock."

Una Grenada wasn't willing to just let that pass. "Did he graduate to high school venues, or what?"

"Our distinguished president, Mr. Morelli, makes that decision," Lou responded, a touch of bitterness in his voice.

At the mere mention of BRAWL's main boss, Joey shook his head in disappointment. If things had gone differently, it could have been him graduating to the next level of wrestling mediocrity. It should have been him.

Milk Shake had no interest in this kind of talk. "Man, forget

Shamrock! Shanty Mick!"

Offended, Scally leaned in. "Hey, hey, Koko B. Ware! Watch with the language!"

Milk Shake simply glared at the wrestling imposter before turning to Lou. "Why is he even here?" he asked, pointing back at Scally.

The blonde menace put his hands on his knees to keep from getting pushed forward and stepped on. "Earnin' my 15%," he shouted defensively.

Una Granada snorted. "Lisch, you're being cheated."

"No room as it is," Milk Shake added, still airing his grievance.

"Enough," Lou shouted, putting his foot down.

But the mayhem was just beginning. Tiny had now arrived. Scraping against the side wall, the 300+ pound behemoth was already huffing and puffing as he inched his way inside. This was getting ridiculous.

"Whoa, my man," Una Grenada cried, trying to keep his ever shrinking space.

Joey's helmet struck the back wall as the others tried to reposition themselves. "Tiny!"

"Damn," Milk Shake simply muttered.

Tiny seemed unaware of the damage his mere presence was inflicting. He just figured everyone had an issue with his tardiness. "Sorry I'm late."

Scally had managed to get pushed to the far side of the room, pinning his face against the wall. "We're sorry you showed up," he griped, his muffled voice barely audible.

"Did somebody order two pies?" Just outside the room was the arrival of another unwelcome visitor.

"Yeah, in here," Lou called out, ignoring the plight of his wrestlers.

WRESTLING WITH JOEYLICIOUS

The pizza delivery guy took a moment to assess his bizarre surroundings before joining the party. Undeterred by the lack of space, he miraculously squirmed his way to Lou's desk.

Joey saw Tiny immediately reach out for the welcome meal. "Tiny, let Lou pay for them first!"

But Tiny already managed to secure an entire pie for himself. Nothing would get between him and his food. Not even his own fingers at times, which had scars of their own from previous feasts devoured in haste.

Una Granada figured as much. "Yeah, slim, save us a slice."

Before the pizza delivery guy could even begin to make his escape, yet another presence appeared at the doorway. The cramped crowd looked over in absolute astonishment as a female hand held up a stack of papers. "Lou, I have something for you to sign."

Lou, as if nothing counterintuitive was going on, just waved her forward. "Okay, Grace. Bring it to my desk."

Grace gave everyone a cold look, but she wasn't about to argue. She had been Lou's secretary far too long to bother. Instead, she obediently made her way through the can of sardines inch by painful inch.

Milk Shake got one of her elbows to his ribs. "Are we supposed to crowd surf her to you? How's she gettin' to the desk?!"

With his face still pressed against the wall, Scally moaned in agony. "Quit shovin'! You're gonna break my neck!"

Ignoring the other occupants as best she could, Grace finally made it to the desk, dropped off the papers, and headed back out. Somehow the pizza delivery guy also managed to squeeze past the exit amidst the hoopla.

When things finally settled and every slice of pizza was wolfed down, Una Grenada turned back to the desk. "So you

~ 111 ~

were saying, Lou?" he said, getting the meeting back on track.

Lou, never one to sugarcoat even the worst of scenarios, broke the news: "Ticket sales for this coming Saturday are looking even bleaker than last week, and those seniors we tangled with are suing the league-"

"We should be suin' them," Milk Shake spat out in disgust.

Una Grenada agreed. "Yeah, some witch broke her cane over my back, and I'm still pulling out the splinters."

"And what about my hospital bill?" Joey chimed in.

"And what about mine comin' after this meeting?" Scally said, adding his voice to the growing resentment.

Lou hushed them all. "Don't worry about the seniors! It's time to focus on this Saturday. I have an idea that should spice things up."

Whenever Lou came up with a new innovative booking plan, the wrestlers held their collective breath. Some laws, undoubtably, were about to be broken. The IRS already had their own drawer of Lou Rossati files, and it was always open. With that being said, the true members of BRAWL welcomed a change whether it was dicey or not. What could possibly be worse than the last few disastrous weeks?

Lou let the tension in the room build. "First off: Lisch, are you cleared to fight?" he finally asked. "I see you're wearing a helmet."

"I'll be ready," Joey responded stoically.

"I didn't ask if you'd be ready. I asked-"

"My client will be in the ring," Scally insisted, immediately shooting down any cause for concern. He wasn't about to lose his cut of $47.50. "Get on with it!"

Lou gave the so-called manager an annoyed look, but decided not to bother pressing him. "Fine. I'm gonna play up the race card in the Joeylicious/Milk Shake match to get us some press."

This was not what everyone had expected. "Where are we? In Minneapolis?" Una Grenada said after a pause.

"Yeah," Milk Shake concurred. "Is he supposed to dress up as a cop or something?"

"How 'bout I dress up as a cop?" Scally retorted, seeing an opening for a cheap shot.

"I'd choke you out before you even got your piece outta the holster," Milk Shale shot back, staring down his little nemesis.

Lou was pleased how things were already shaping up. "Okay, this is all good stuff. Keep spit-balling."

"If Lisch is still ailing, why don't I just fight Milk Shake?" Tiny said, talking around his last mouthful of pizza. "I'm white, too."

Lou thought about that for a second, but ultimately disagreed. "The Italian/Black angle is a bit more primal. But you can fight the Dominican."

Una Grenada looked up from a pizza stain on his pants. "Puerto Rican!"

Lou shrugged at the correction. "We're fighting at Our Lady of Grace. Does it make a difference?"

Joey would have wrestled King Kong if it meant keeping his streak alive. "Well, I'm down for whatever. What's the plan?"

Chapter 17

Milk Shakes, Payoffs & Young Guns

Milk Shake entered his apartment more bruised from a meeting than from any of his recent matches. It had been a long day, so he was not ready for what waited for him as he stepped into the kitchen. Sitting at the table with her arms folded was his girlfriend, Charlene. There was a delicious but cold looking meal laid out in front of her, and romantic candles were burnt all the way down to the base. Charlene glared at her man with both anger and sorrow.

Milk Shake sat down cautiously and gave her an awkward smile. "Hey, baby. Sorry I'm late."

Charlene gritted her teeth. "For our anniversary dinner?"

"Has it been six months already?"

"Two years! I've been cooking all day!"

"It's not like we're married or anything." Milk Shake's hole was quickly becoming too big to climb out of.

Charlene pursed her lips and narrowed her eyes as this was the one subject they had gone over exhaustively. It obviously wasn't her fault that their relationship hadn't progressed. "I'll pretend I didn't hear that."

"Okay, listen..." Milk Shake leaned forward and pulled on one of her hands.

Charlene pulled away, unwilling to let him touch her. If he

was going to smooth talk his way out of this one, she would not lend a hand.

Milk Shake rethought his approach. "I will make this up to you. I promise," he said, trying to placate her. "Lou called a last minute meeting. There was nothin' I could do." Clearly that wasn't smooth enough.

"Are you really bringing up your wrestling as an excuse? A meeting, no less!" Charlene was beside herself.

"You know this is important to me," he shot back, standing his ground.

"Honey, you have a real job now. You work for the city. Can you please give up on this professional athlete pipe dream?" If the pissed off approach wasn't working, she would try the practical one.

Milk Shake frowned and sat back. "You see?! This is what pisses me off!"

Charlene leaned forward. "You were a basketball player in college! Division III! Okay, so you tore up your knee, but you weren't getting drafted anyway." She kindly left out the fact that her boyfriend rode the bench in college, and tore up his knee running to a practice he was late for.

"The NBA has a D-League now. I could've been a walk-on." Milk Shake also conveniently left out the previous fact.

"You moved your stuff in eight months ago," she said, bringing them back on topic. "When are we going to make this official?"

Having already lost the argument at jump street, he decided to play dumb. "Whatta we talkin' about again?"

Charlene scoffed. Her true anger was about to erupt as she thought of the next line she would scream. Finally, she just threw her linen napkin in her man's face, and stormed off to the bedroom.

WRESTLING WITH JOEYLICIOUS

Milk Shake picked the napkin up as he heard the bedroom door lock. Obviously, he would be sleeping on the couch this night... and several nights hereafter.

* * * * *

Lou had spent many Wednesday nights at his local dive bar, so he felt right at home conducting shady business here. It was the kind of seedy establishment in which one could get completely drunk for just $20. And from the look of the surrounding clientele, many twenty-dollar bills had already been spent.

Other than Lou, the only other patron still sitting upright was the greasy little man sitting next to him. This could have been Lou's brother, but he was just a reporter for the Canarsie Courier. The Canarsie Courier was basically a high school paper written by adults who weren't talented enough to write for their high school paper at the time they were in high school. The reporter sitting next to Lou settled for a General Education Diploma, better known as a G.E.D.

But Lou knew how to milk this. If he played his cards right, BRAWL could still be saved. The reporter salivated at the sight of the white envelop already sitting on the bar. Well, maybe not the envelop so much, but the cash peeking out from inside.

This was all part of Lou's plan as he placed his glass next to the visible cash. "Remember the time I helped you with that problem?"

The reporter looked up from the cash. "No, not really." He was honestly confused.

Lou had the reporter's attention, and that was all that mattered. "Well, I would help you if you ever had one," he said, conceding that he hadn't actually done anything to help the man in the past.

"Just gimme the cash." The reporter wasn't interested in mind games.

Lou smiled, looked around as if any of the surrounding drunks were actually watching, and carefully slid the envelop over - the cash shifting every so slightly during its journey.

The reporter quickly grabbed the envelope and shoved it into his pocket before any prying eyes could notice. Once again, there were no prying eyes - just foggy, glazed over ones. But now the reporter would have to count the pitiful sum he was actually handed in private after the meeting. And that was all Lou had intended with his cloak and dagger act.

"And you're tight with your editor?" Lou continued, feeling confident. "You can get us a front page?"

The reporter's eyes finished darting around the room, paranoia finally running its course. "It's the Canarsie Courier, Lou. I'm not even sure we have an editor." This was true. The Courier's last editor died three years ago, and still hadn't been replaced. It took two years before anyone had realized the editor had actually died. This was not a tight run ship.

Lou waved his hand in frustration. "Just get it done, alright?!"

Feeling like he had gained equally from their suspect encounter, the reporter held up his glass. "Cheers." The money was good, but with Lou there was always a possibility that bigger, more lucrative crimes could pay off down the line.

Lou looked at him suspiciously. It wasn't like the reporter to make a toast after this kind of transaction, but there was no reason not to join him. Holding up his own glass, they toasted and downed their drinks. The reporter then took off, leaving Lou to his own thoughts. The future of BRAWL was starting

WRESTLING WITH JOEYLICIOUS

to look brighter. Or darker. Depending on one's point of view.

* * * * *

Joey stood in front of a volleyball net which was set up for his seventh grade gym class. His students were clearly confused. On one hand, they were looking at a volley ball net; on the other, their teacher was wearing a batting helmet. Yes, believe it or not, Joey still couldn't get that pesky chunk of plastic off. And he tried everything: butter, cooking oil, powdered donuts; that sucker was stuck - and good.

The awkward silence hanging in the air was abruptly broken by Scally's unexpected arrival. Wearing street clothes, he strolled up to Joey as if the kids weren't even there. "You actually slept in that thing?"

Joey glared at the direct cause of just that fact. "I can't get it off!" It took a second before he realized that there was now a bigger problem at hand. "Why are you here? Father Randazzo reinstated you?"

Scally stuck his hands in his pockets. "No, but I need him to. I have these two chicks I'm workin', and no scratch to take them out."

"What two chicks?" Joe asked, ignoring his class.

The class was intrigued by this sort of adult talk. And one of the youngsters, in particular, would not be ignored. "Ha, ha! The loser's on unemployment!"

Scally turned on the prepubescent wise ass like a whip. "No, the city won't let me collect! I wasn't workin' here long enough. You believe that, kids?" he continued, addressing everyone.

"Apparently, our elected officials are even more corrupt than you," one of the more pragmatic students said, chiming in.

WRESTLING WITH JOEYLICIOUS

The middle-aged degenerate frowned. "Well, I don't know about that."

Joey waved his knucklehead friend away. "Would you get outta here?! You're gonna get me in trouble now!"

"Can't I just hang? I have nothing else to do." Scally wasn't fooling. The bars didn't open til noon.

The seventh graders couldn't see their teacher roll his eyes under the helmet, but they did hear him sigh. "Fine. But if Father Randazzo walks in, I don't know you."

Scally laughed. "He's not gonna buy that."

"Then just go already!" Joey was itching to demonstrate a devastating wrestling move on someone. Guess who?

"Relax. He's workin' a funeral," Scally replied. "We're in the clear." Apparently, that settled the matter.

But there was still that initial confusion between Joey and his students that needed to be settled, and one of the twerps finally steered the class back on track: "Why is the volleyball net up if we're playing baseball?"

Mr. Cassata suddenly remembered that he had a class to teach. "Who said we're playing baseball?" he shot back, quickly defending his syllabus.

"Duh. Your batting helmet," the same twerp retorted.

The unqualified teacher shook his head. "Don't worry about my batting helmet." He picked up a volleyball. "Whattaya call this?" he asked the class.

Joey was clearly trying to deflect any and all inquires into his ridiculous look, but there was a class clown amongst his flock who would not be deterred. The kid's grandfather wore an eye patch, and liked to play Bingo from time to time. "I heard you got your ass kicked by an old man."

This got a round of laughter from the entire class.

Joey glared at them. "Quiet," he shouted. "It was a cheap

shot from behind - like Pat Garrett and Billy the Kid."

"Who's Billy the Kid?" one of the amused students asked.

Scally looked at the ignorant child incredulously. "You never saw Young Guns?"

The seventh graders must have thought their former instructor was referring to some obscure black-and-white film. Of course, they hadn't even been born yet when the 1988 Brat Pack western shined on the big screen. They couldn't pick Emilio Estevez or Lou Diamond Phillips out of a police line-up.

Joey figured this was a teaching moment just the same. "Actually, Billy the Kid got shot in Young Guns II."

"Yeah, but he didn't die," Scally shot back. "Remember he was that old dude tellin' the story in the end?"

Joey paused before nodding. "Oh, yeah."

Now the students were even more lost. One of them broke through the haze cackling. "Hey, I'm Billy! I'm a kid!"

The others cracked up again, until Scally snatched the volleyball from Joey and fired it at little Billy. The ball ricochetted off Billy's forehead with such force, that it literally flew over the net for a point. Any soccer player would have been proud. "Game on! Bunch'a twerps!" Scally wasn't playing around.

That shut the seventh graders up.

Sniffing with bravado as if he had just won a significant battle, Scally turned back to his one wrestling client. "You know, I think that helmet can actually work for ya."

Joey's forehead wrinkled with intrigue. "For the Milk Shake match?"

"A change of pace never hurt anyone." It was the most profound bit of advice his manager ever uttered.

Joey reflected on his recent hospital stay. There was a lot a

WRESTLING WITH JOEYLICIOUS

wrestler could do to mix things up for the better. It had certainly worked wonders for Mick Foley and his three alter egos. His mind raced as he considered the possibilities. "Yeah, like when Mick Foley became Mankind...," Joey finally muttered, revealing his thoughts.

"Ah, ya see?" Scally beamed. "Now you're thinkin'!"

Chapter 18

Gehrig's Ghost

Several BRAWL participants sat across a long table that was setup for a press conference. Yes, you heard that right. Joey and Scally sat at one end, while Milk Shake and Charlene sat on the other. Lou sat between the two parties, looking like a man who was very proud of himself, though he was finding it hard to look at his Italian Dream. Joey had added an old fashioned 1930s New York Yankees uniform to go along with his batting helmet; gone was his signature black singlet and red boa. In front of them were a few local reporters all with questions about the upcoming event. Among them, of course, was Lou's main sleaze from The Canarsie Courier. In fairness to the Courier's representative, though, the representatives of the other affiliates were equally third rate.

Behind the reporters were the fourth graders of Our Lady of Grace. After all, this "press conference" was occurring in their school's cafeteria. It was difficult enough to keep the youngsters' attention at the best of times; they had absolutely no interest in what was happening here.

A reporter for The Daily Challenge was the first to jump into the subdued fray. "Mr. Rossati, why have this press conference in a grammar school cafeteria?"

Lou forced a smile. It was a good question, but not where he wanted to start. "Saturday night's event will take place in this school's gym, and these kids are our target audience."

WRESTLING WITH JOEYLICIOUS

A reporter from King's Plaza News held up a hand. "Who else does your audience normally consist of?"

That wasn't a question Lou wanted to hear or answer either, but he couldn't just ignore it. He forced an even wider smile. "Priests and nuns... some seniors. But we're open to everyone." He saw an opportunity to get the young audience involved. "So kids: tell your parents, tell your brothers and sisters, spread the word," he called out to them enthusiastically.

Crickets. Few of the fourth graders even knew that they were being spoken to.

Realizing this was where he needed to start earning Lou's pittance of a bribe, Canarsie Courier held up his hand. "Joeylicious, do you have anything against blacks?" he asked quite innocently.

Looking over at Milk Shake, Joey was somewhat confused. "No, not-"

Scally slammed his elbow into his wrestler's ribs.

Suddenly, Joey remembered what they had discussed at the incredibly cramped meeting, and pivoted. "On Saturday night I do! Who said they can wrestle, anyway? Can they play basketball? Fine. Football? Sure."

"Track and field," Scally added, trying to second his client's motion. He ended up undermining it.

Joey looked over, his flow interrupted. "I'll give them that, too."

"Cricket," the blonde distraction added. Again.

"I'm talking about this country." Joey was getting frustrated now.

"Those dark-skinned black guys play cricket in Marine park every weekend." The manager had a point, but still.

Joey sneered. "Okay, cricket. Whatever."

Scally wasn't done yet. "Boxing?"

~ 123 ~

WRESTLING WITH JOEYLICIOUS

Milk Shake was tired of the nonsensical back and forth, and shined the spotlight his way. "Damn straight! When was the last time you saw a white guy beat a black man in the ring?"

Joey slammed his hands on the table. "Haven't you ever heard of Rocky Balboa?! He beat Apollo to win the title in Rocky II!"

"Yeah baby, 'Eye of the Tiger,'" Scally chimed in. He went to give his best bud a high five, but Joey wasn't having it.

"No Scal, that's Rocky III."

Scally brushed that off, and turned to his African-American nemesis. "And that's when he whipped that chump, Mr. T's ass, Chocolate Milk Shake!"

Milk Shake shot up from his chair. "Yeah, but don't forget that Mr. T killed Rocky's little white manager right before the fight!"

Canarsie Courier knew his question planted the seed of controversy, but now he needed another one to make it bloom. "Milk Shake, is it true that Joeylicious slept with your wife?"

Charlene, of course, was immediately offended. "Excuse me?!"

Milk Shake hesitantly looked over at his better half. "Actually, we're not married." Naturally, he chose the worst possible response.

"Engaged?" a reporter from The Bay Current asked, hoping for clarification.

Milk Shake was clearly uncomfortable with the direction the conference was heading. "No, we're just dating currently," he reiterated, sprinkling dirt on his grave.

Charlene's expression let her man know that he was in serious trouble when they got home. Or in the car on the way home. Maybe even during the walk to the car from the table. Either way, Milk Shake was royally screwed.

WRESTLING WITH JOEYLICIOUS

"But you plan on proposing soon?" a member of Kings County Press pressed.

Milk Shake, already dead and buried, was fed up with his futile attempts at diffusing the bomb. So he just yanked out all the colored wires at once. "We're livin' together, alright?! Give a brother some space up in here!"

"Do you think maybe you should finish answering that initial question?" Charlene's controlled tone masked her seething anger.

"What initial-" Milk Shake suddenly realized where his focus should have been. "Oh. Right. Nah, Liscious ain't bangin' my wife-"

Like Scally with Joey, Charlene elbowed her own wrestler in the ribs.

"I mean, girlfriend," Milk Shake shouted, making the quick incorrect correction.

Charlene's elbow was far more brutal the second time.

Scally figured it was about time he added fuel to the four alarm fire, and stood up. "Yeah, that's because I am!"

Milk Shake's head spun around in a fury. "I'll kill him," he screeched. Knocking over his chair, he made a quick dash toward the blonde menace but the architect of the mayhem grabbed him just in time.

"Take it easy," Lou whispered in his wrestler's ear. "This is working out perfectly! He's just playing the part!"

Milk Shake pushed Lou away, and sat back down, his ire and loathing for Joey's best friend barely contained.

Another reporter rose a hand. "Hi. Don Simmons, Brooklyn Daily Eagle," he began before being recognized. "Joeylicious, I see you have a helmet on. Is this part of a new persona? Formally, the 'Italian Dream,' now the 'Italian Helmet?'"

A couple of reporters chuckled as Joey took the question in

stride. "In case you haven't noticed, I'm also wearing a Yankees jersey."

"And what's the significance of that?" Brooklyn Daily Eagle pressed.

"Saturday night, Scally and I will be introducing you all to the alter ego of Joeylicious." How's that for burying the lead?

Milk Shake's head spun again. "What?!"

"Aren't we doin' the introduction now?" Scally asked, trying to correct his client. "You're already in costume."

"I haven't worked out the voice yet," Joey elaborated with his hand over the mic.

Scally nodded. "So we'll work on that later."

Joey mulled that over.

Brooklyn Daily Eagle continued with his probing. Intrigue was now in the air. "Joey, you were saying?"

Ready to address all witnesses, Joey's smile widened. "Ladies and gentlemen, I give you...," He stood up dramatically with his arms outstretched, "...Gehrig's Ghost!" He turned proudly to let everyone see the #4 on the back of his jersey.

"C'mon, man," Milk Shake muttered. It was bad enough he had to deal with Charlene later, but now this.

Bay Current was interested in learning more. "Why Lou Gehrig?" This was worth a full paragraph on page nine of the failing paper at least. Okay, maybe page 11.

Scally gave the reporter an obvious look. "Because of his streak."

But Bay Current wanted clarification. "So he doesn't have ALS, or anything?"

That went right over Joey's head. He was only thinking of the press getting this part right: "I haven't missed a match in 20 years."

WRESTLING WITH JOEYLICIOUS

"Yeah, but about the ALS," Bay Current continued, pressing for that page nine or 11 story.

Milk Shake was still stewing. "He drops a bomb like this..."

Charlene, seeing how upset this was making her man, softened as she took his hand. "It's okay, baby."

Daily Challenge caught the heartfelt exchange and chuckled. "He shook up the Milk Shake."

Brooklyn Daily Eagle, refusing to be distracted by the couple's apparent reconciliation, pointed his tape recorder at the wrestler formerly known as Joeylicious. "Gehrig's Ghost: other than your outfit, what's the difference between you and Joeylicious?"

This caught Joey off guard. It was not a question he and Scally had anticipated. "Well, Joeylicious is vicious and delicious; Gehrig's Ghost is...," he stammered in search of difference, "...vicious, delicious and..."

Scally saw that his client was flailing, and jumped in for the save: "Safety conscious."

Realizing that things were getting away from him, Lou hoped to bring the focus of the press back to where he wanted it to be. "Can we get back to the racial questions, please? This lunch period ends in five minutes."

Scally leaned over to Joey, tingling with anticipation. "Things are gonna be rockin' on Saturday!"

Joey smiled. "Oh, yeah!"

Chapter 19

Race War!

Despite what Joey and Scally had been expecting, things were not rocking at Our Lady of Grace's gymnasium that Saturday night. It was pretty much the same scarce, lowlife crowd as usual. Lowlife was fine; Scarce: not so much. But this was not the time for BRAWL tears. The show went on.

In the ring, doing their best to ignore the low turnout, Joey's new persona, Gehrig's Ghost, and his opponent Milk Shake were mid battle. Joey had gone all in with his new alter ego. Besides the undersized batting helmet and old fashioned Yankees uniform, he had even included steel spikes for the match.

Scally's cheers echoed throughout the near empty chamber as he held up two large Styrofoam cups of beer from the back row of the bleachers. Charlene sat a few rows ahead of him, embarrassed at the fact that she was even there. But her boyfriend wasn't completely useless, so she bared it. At least Milk Shake had a real job during the week. Whoever dated this Gehrig's Ghost character, would really have relationship issues.

Lou paced the floor nervously, his eyes continuously darting to the gym's entrance. Where the hell was everybody? So far, it looked like Canarsie Courier had really screwed the pooch. The $19.50 Lou had stuffed into that white envelop might have covered the reporter's Wednesday night drinking tab, but it

WRESTLING WITH JOEYLICIOUS

wasn't doing much here.

Milk Shake was starting to get distracted as well. "Lisch, there's no one here," he said, sharing his concern with his opponent. "How long should we keep this goin'?" His eyes kept going to Charlene, her arms folded in boredom.

Gehrig's Ghost straightened in confusion. "Who's Lisch?"

Milk Shake refrained from scoffing at BRAWL's newest member. "I mean, Gehrig's Ghost! This is embarrassing, man!"

Gehrig's Ghost had also lost hope, but he wasn't about to lose the match. "Should I just pin you now?"

Milk Shake tensed up. "Pin me?! Don't you mean, pin you?"

Gehrig's Ghost frowned. "You beat me last time!"

"And you beat me the three times before that," Milk Shake shot back.

"What is this? The best four outta seven? I just had an injury! This is my comeback match!" Things were getting complicated.

"Gehrig's Ghost never even fought before," Milk Shake reasoned.

"Exactly! You expect him to lose in his debut?" It was here that Gehrig's Ghost had finally stuck his landing. A wrestler never lost his first match, unless that wrestler was preordained to lose every match thereafter. Did anyone want Gehrig's Ghost to be the next Brooklyn Brawler? That guy hardly even landed a punch in the glory days of the WWF.

Milk Shake was done arguing. He just wanted to go home and curl up with his girlfriend while she was still his girlfriend. "Whatever, man," he conceded. Then he let Gehrig's Ghost execute a devastating move that should have ended his misery. But when the spirit of the great Yankee jumped on him for the pin, a commotion erupted outside the ring. Milk Shake took

WRESTLING WITH JOEYLICIOUS

advantage of the welcome distraction, and kicked out before the ref could count to three.

Storming through the gym's entrance was a stream of black activists led by Ulysses S. Compton, the biggest rabble-rouser of them all. He was basically the Al Sharpton of Brooklyn before big Al lost the weight for TV. Ulysses and his gang shouted their displeasures as they carried signs protesting Gehrig's Ghost, and the legitimacy of the match in general.

Lou finally stopped pacing and smiled. Things were back on schedule.

The new arrivals even peaked Charlene's interest. "Oh, it's on now!" She jumped up from her seat. "C'mon, baby! Kick some old baseball player ass!"

Milk Shake brought his attention back to Gehrig's Ghost and shrugged. "Sorry, GG. My peeps are here. It can't be helped."

It was obvious Gehrig's Ghost hadn't quite grasped what was happening. "What? Wait-"

Too late. Milk Shake was already pounding on him.

Joey's alternate persona was near tears as he looked out at his one loyal fan who also happened to be his manager in the audience. "Where are my peeps?"

As if he had been summoned, Mick Foley suddenly appeared in the corner of the ring. "We're back!"

Gehrig's Ghost's heart fluttered. Not only was the Micker at his side, but Dude Love, Cactus Jack, and Mankind also appeared in the other corners of the ring. This was the best fan base he could ever ask for.

But Mick and his boys weren't there to blindly support their understudy. "Joey, it's time to answer for some copyright laws you've infringed upon."

Gehrig's Ghost frowned from under Milk Shake's choke hold. "Whattaya mean?"

WRESTLING WITH JOEYLICIOUS

Mick leaned forward. "I'm the only wrestler who is allowed multiple personas!"

Milk Shake, confused by who or what Gehrig's Ghost was talking to, released the strange wrestler and stepped back. Seeing their opening, all four of Mick's personas then charged forward and wailed on Joey's alter ego.

Unexpectedly, Mrs. Cassata entered the gym behind Ulysses's last activist, and immediately looked with concern toward the ring. She saw what everyone else in the audience saw: Joey/Gehrig's Ghost swinging his arms around like a madman at nothing but air. He even dropped to the canvas a few times as if he had been hit.

Milk Shake, now even more concerned than Mrs. Cassata, took another step back and practically hid behind the ropes for cover.

Ulysses could only shake his head. "This white boy's crazy."

Mrs. Cassata heard that remark, but her eyes were focused on her son. Unfortunately, she agreed with the disrupter's assessment, and now she was going to have to climb into the ring and save Joey from himself.

But before Mrs. Cassata could take a step in that direction, another crowd burst through the front entrance. This time it was a bunch of Italian Mafioso types led by Capo Johnny Carbone - basically John Gotti in a cheaper suit. The mobbed up mob carried pro-Joeylicious/Gehrig's Ghost signs as they shouted out their support for a fellow Italian. Lou smiled again - an even bigger one this time. He loved it when a plan came together.

Carbone took notice of the nutty baseball player his crew was there to root for. "What the hell is he doin'?"

Gehrig's Ghost had just taken another blow from imaginary Mankind when he caught sight of the latest arrivals. "My peeps," he beamed.

Mick and his alter egos suddenly vanished just as quickly as they had appeared. Reinvigorated, it was about time Gehrig's Ghost had another swing at Milk Shake.

Carbone saw the fire in Gehrig's Ghost's eyes. "Alright," he cheered.

Ulysses was clearly confused. "What just happened?"

The wrestlers were back on an even canvas. Just going through the motions halfheartedly before, they now went all out as if a championship belt was at stake. Of course, it wasn't, because Lou was too cheap to buy one in the first place. But the two combatants fought like mad dogs just the same, Milk Shake eventually gaining the upper hand.

After receiving a brutal blow from his lanky rival, Gehrig's Ghost flew out of the ring, smashing his head on the hardwood floor. The sound of the helmet cracking helped him regain his senses. Joey jumped up and felt the gym's stale breeze flow through his greasy hair. He looked down in relieved amazement, and saw the shattered helmet lying at his feet. With a roar, the non-mobbed up Italian ripped off the old Yankee uniform to reveal a black singlet and red cape underneath. Joeylicious was reborn!

"Yeah," Scally cried out, throwing up a celebratory hand. Of course, beer sloshed out of his Styrofoam cup, spilling onto poor Charlene.

Carbone went back to being perplexed. "Who's this guy now?"

His lieutenant raised a curious eyebrow as well. "Boss, are those highlights in his hair? I thought he was Italian."

Carbone could only shrug.

"Milk Shake, get that white boy," Ulysses shouted, standing closer to the action.

WRESTLING WITH JOEYLICIOUS

As if following orders, Milk Shake climbed to the top rope, and dove out of the ring, crashing down on his opponent.

But Joeylicious recovered quickly. He could see much better without that annoying helmet in his eyes, and Milk Shake paid the price. Furious blows in rapid-fire fashion were equally exchanged between the fighters until the ref had something to say: "Double count out!"

"It's a draw," Scally shouted, taking umbrage with the human zebra.

"Or draw. Whichever," the ref said, dismissing the drunk fan.

Both camps of supporters responded with boos and cheers alike.

Joeylicious and Milk Shake struggled to their feet only to look at each other and smile. Hand in hand they simultaneously threw up their arms in victorious solidarity. It was easily the best fight they had ever had.

Carbone approached Ulysses. "I guess we'll both get 'em next time. Huh, Ulysses?"

"Yeah, John. Good to see you," Ulysses replied. "Let's do lunch some time."

"Call my office."

"You got it."

And the two neighborhood rivals headed to the exit as friends.

Scally was still jumping up and down on the bleachers, yelling at anyone who would listen until he saw a not-so friendly face staring up at him.

Mrs. Cassata was absolutely fuming at the drunken sight.

The blonde menace held up both Styrofoam cups. "What? They're ginger ales," he said defensively.

"Find yourself another place to sleep," Mrs. Cassata shot

back. "Forever." At that, she turned and marched toward the ring.

"Mrs. C, c'mon," Scally desperately called out. "It's cold outside for May!"

Joey heard his friend's pleas, and turned from his bonding moment with Milk Shake to his mother suddenly standing directly in front of him. She was none too pleased. "Ma! You came," he cried, shaking off the initial shock of her presence.

She immediately smacked her son upside the head. Without waiting for a complaint, she then grabbed Joey's ear and dragged him out of the gym like a child.

Lou watched the short-lived domestic dispute with amusement. Shaking his head and laughing, he was suddenly looking forward to his Saturday nights again. "BRAWL," he muttered to himself with pride.

Something off to the side caught his attention, and Lou turned to see his reporter from The Canarsie Courier sitting in the bleachers. The reporter held up the front page of tomorrow's newspaper.

There in large black and white print was what Lou had been hoping for:

BRAWL WRESTLES WITH RACIAL TENSIONS

Chapter 20

The Flying Irishman

Holding out hope for a two star Yelp rating but stuck on a star and a half, the diner was your typical after hour Brooklyn eatery. Scattered downtrodden patrons sat at wobbly tables decorated with plastic flowers, the waitresses had bad hair and few teeth, and the specials were off limits to the human stomach. You either ordered a cheeseburger deluxe here, or the underpaid chef in the back handed you a metaphorical gun to play Russian Roulette with.

Sitting at one of the booths, attacking their food with gusto, were Joey, Una Grenada and Milk Shake, all dressed in their post-match attire. For once they were upbeat about their pitiful athletic careers. The eventful night at BRAWL sparked their conversation along with their appetite.

Tiny was present with his three wrestling companions, but he sat alone at his own booth sluggishly devouring his unjust desserts. He chose to sit alone not only for the obvious geometrical reasons due to his size, which expanded with each terrifying bite, but for the solitude. Tiny was depressed. And his double cheeseburger deluxe order was paying the price.

Scally entered the suspect establishment with his head on a swivel. Spotting Joey and the boys, he made a beeline for their booth. Joey was sitting next to Una Grenada, so the blonde imp was forced to plop down next to Milk Shake. He paid no mind to the dirty look he got from his rival. "What up, fellas?" he asked as much as stated.

Milk Shake scooted over as much as he could. "That cop let you go? Would'a shot my ass."

Joey looked between them with confusion. "What cop?"

Una Grenada laughed, pointing at Scally. "He pissed on 5-0 after your match with Milk Shake."

Joey's eyes went wide. "He did wh-" Instead of asking his fellow wrestlers, he turned and looked directly at the culprit. "You did what?!"

"He was plainclothes. It was an accident." Of course, this made all the difference to Scally. If he was going to urinate on an officer of the law, he would make damn sure the officer was off duty.

Incredulously, Joey narrowed his eyes. "How was it an accident?!"

"The line for the bathroom was out the door! So I went behind the bleachers. But I had a half a hard-on, so my stream arched, and I got his pants from under the seat." The human hand grenade thought this settled the issue, but it only opened the door for more alarming queries.

The only follow-up question Joey could muster was an open mouthed gawk.

With no more room to slide over other than through the wall, Milk Shake could no longer even look at the innocent giver of golden showers. "Why would you have a boner watching an all-male wrestling match?"

"Well, technically I was done watchin'," Scally said to the table before turning to his booth mate. "But my thing's got a mind of its own. I gotta explain this to a black guy?"

"Yeah, you kind'a do," Milk Shake shot back, now offended as much as disgusted.

Joey reached desperately for a silver lining. "At least you can only get banned from my corner once."

"Yeah, now they extended my ban to the venues," Scally sighed, correcting his client.

This was another serious blow to Joey's already floundering career. They had been planning a big marketing push for months. "Which venues?"

"All of them," his manager answered, shrugging casually. "But only temporarily."

Joey held back his mounting fury. "Define temporarily?"

Scally looked around for a waitress or an escape pod. "Three months," he finally clarified. This was the last thing Joey wanted to hear, and he knew it. It was only a matter of time before the table between them would be overturned, leaving him defenseless.

Joey agreed with his manager's assessment. "It's memorabilia night at Saint Dom's next week! Who's gonna man my table?!" Ah, memorabilia night: Christmas to the wrestlers of BRAWL. Where else could one peddle useless junk to non-existent fans? Their weekly pay of $47.50 before expenses would easily spike to 54 or even $55. And that was if things were slow! The potential for a financial windfall staggered the mind of the mindless.

"Is that all you can think of?" Scally bemoaned. There was honest to goodness pain in his voice.

Joey decided to doubled down. He let a lot slide, but he had his limits. "My order of 'Bring the Violence' buttons just came in!"

That did it. With no argument to counter with and no one else to turn to, Scally pulled out his trump card: the blame game. "I was wrongfully detained! My beef with the authorities goes back to that White Lion concert in '91!" This was a constant gripe of Scally's over the years. He was thrown out of the once famous Brooklyn rock club, L'Amour, for attempting to climb the stage. Scally told the cops that Vito Bratta, the flashy lead guitarist of White Lion, had asked him for managerial advice and a cold beer before starting his solo. The cops didn't buy it, and L'Amour never heard from Scally or Vito Bratta again.

Joey, exasperated, flopped back in his seat. He was at a loss, until he thought of how best to sum up his manager's failings. "First you're fired, then my mom throws you out, and now you're banned from all gyms. You're like a triple threat to all that's holy."

Now a silver lining dawned on Scally. "At least I'm battin' 1,000."

Joey flashed the blonde menace a final look of disgust before getting up. "I'm sitting with Tiny!" Grabbing his cheese fries, he would let Milk Shake and Una Grenada deal with matters that really didn't matter.

Clearly unfazed by his friend's exit, Scally had bigger fish to fry. His buzz was wearing off, and he couldn't possibly eat in this place sober. He grabbed Milk Shake's glass of water, and before the lanky wrestler could even protest, abruptly emptied it into the cheap vase holding the table's fake, sun-bleached flowers. He then pulled out a hidden bottle of beer from his inside coat pocket, and poured it into the glass.

The foam was bubbling over the rim, when Scally lifted the glass to his lips. Before he could satisfy his unquenchable thirst, though, a sixty-year-old waitress going on 80 interrupted the Irish ritual.

"Can I get you any-" She adjusted her glasses, noticed the beer foam dribbling onto the table, and frowned at the scrawny rule breaker.

The lush looked up innocently, but knew the waitress had

put two and two together and came up with the alcoholic beverage in his glass. "Quit crowdin' me, princess," he protested, quickly turning the tables on her like only he could. "I'll ring for ya when I finish my apple spritzer."

The waitress gladly obliged, and a sound of distaste rose from one of the wrestlers at the booth. Scally turned to the only man that utterance of annoyance could have possibly came from. "Milk Shake, you ever bang an Asian broad?"

The African-American's disbelief was evident. "What?!"

Not realizing that this was an unwelcome topic, the politically incorrect deviant shifted and dove right into what he was thinking. "Here's my theory: my equipment is to Asian women what yours is to white women."

Una Grenada scoffed and shook his head. "Man, you crazy!"

"Think about it." Somewhere down the deep, dark crevices of Scally's little mind, he had a point.

The Puerto Rican wrestler felt excluded. "And what am I packing in relation to white women?" he asked, hesitantly playing along.

Scally thought about that for a second. He should have taken a full minute. "You're somewhere between me and Milk Shake."

At that point, and at many points prior, Milk Shake would have done anything to shut Scally up. "Finish your apple spritzer!" If only he was carrying a blunt instrument. "Tired of hearin' your ass."

Suddenly, Scally's attention was drawn elsewhere as two women entered the diner and slid into a nearby booth. He leaned forward. "Well, well, what have we here?" he announced with relished sleaze.

One of the women was rather tall, but her stunning red hair was eye catching. Scally wasn't the least bit interested. Her companion was Asian. He tapped on the table. "Gentlemen, if you'd excuse me."

Welcoming the respite, neither of the wrestlers got in the way of Scally or his beer's departure. They knew he would go down in flames, and they would gladly watch from a distance.

As Scally reached the women's table, it was clear that the redhead was as tall sitting down as he was standing up. But again: he wasn't interested in her. Her shorter companion was Asian. He gestured toward the sad flowers resting on their table. "Ladies! I hope you like the flowers I left out for ya."

The redhead was stoic as she took in the blonde annoyance, then the flowers, then the rest of the diner. "There are flowers on every table," she said deadpan, making her point.

As if to explain, Scally held out his arms, and sloshed some beer on the floor. "I didn't know where you were gonna sit."

The redhead rolled her eyes, and Scally took that as an invitation to sit next to her friend. It wasn't. "Hello! No one invited you to-"

He threw red a wink. "Don't mention it." Then he turned his full attention to "you know who." "Hey, hot stuff, any relation to Washi or Sayo?"

The Asian woman was understandably confused. "Who?"

"Just a shot in the dark." Even Scally knew he was reaching here.

The redhead was already tired of his act. "They aren't all related, you know?"

Turning that back on her, Scally gave red a look of exaggerated shock. "'They?' That sounds a tad racist to me."

Now red was mad. "Is there a point to you being here?"

"I just had a question for your lovely friend," the scrawny tornado said quite innocently. This bought him a moment of staying power with the Asian woman at least. "Have you ever been with a black man?" he asked, quickly ending her suspense.

Quite understandably, the Asian woman gasped before her mouth turned down. "Excuse me?!"

The redhead crumpled up her linen napkin, and fired it at the table intruder. "You get the hell away from us!"

Well immune to idle threats, Scally kept his eyes on what he thought was the prize. "Here's my two cents: I can be your bridge to a man of color."

The Asian woman was less confused now, but still pretended this was a bad dream. "What bridge?" she still managed to ask.

"Well, you can't just go from an Asian guy to a black guy. That's plain harsh. But someone like myself - I could offer you smooth passage." He was almost philosophical.

* * * * *

Joey plopped his cheese fries down forcefully as he roughly took a seat across from Tiny. His annoyance at Scally quickly disappeared as he regarded the large wrestler who was eating far less enthusiastically than usual. After watching him for a moment, Joey decided to voice his concern: "Tiny, what's wrong?"

Tiny looked up at Joey with his eyes shrouded in defeat. He couldn't find the words, though, so his attention went right back to his food. Even he was surprised that his cheeseburgers were still standing.

Trying to coax the gentle giant into expressing himself, Joey stuck his toe into his emotional water. "Okay, so you lost again. Somebody's gotta take it on the chin for BRAWL."

Shoving the rest of one of the burgers into his mouth kept Tiny from opening up - his heart that is.

WRESTLING WITH JOEYLICIOUS

"Are you upset they're out of onion rings?" Joey asked, continuing to pry cautiously.

Tiny continued to sulk as he chewed.

"Would you spit it out already?" his wrestling mate finally shouted, pulling the band-aid off in frustration.

The big man sighed heavily. "I have two boys," he said, finally coming clean. "Twins."

This took Joey by surprise. "I didn't even know you were married."

"Divorced," Tiny clarified.

"Whatta you do for a living, Tiny?" Joey was enthralled. Who was this mountain of mystery?

Tiny suddenly lit up as if he was on automatic pilot, surprising Joey even more: "CEO of a hedge fund. I specialize in mortgage lending, debt financing and have an eye toward derivatives in the future. I'm even considering merging with-"

Holding up his hands, the financial idiot cried mercy. "Tiny: you lost me at hedge fund."

The 300+ pounder refocused. His concerns had nothing to do with business. "Anyway, next Saturday my boys turn eight."

Joey knew where this was going. "And you'd like to give them a proper birthday present?" he asked as much as stated.

"Something like that." Tiny was relieved that someone understood his plight.

"So your boys have never seen you wrestle?" the Italian cheese fry pressed.

"They've been dying to, but- I always have to get my ass kicked, and take the fall." And this was the heart of the matter.

"So next week will be the exception," Joey quickly announced. The solution seemed simple enough.

Tiny gave his counselor a look of renewed sorrow. "How?"

WRESTLING WITH JOEYLICIOUS

Neither of the men reacted as an airborne Scally suddenly flew past their booth and crashed into a cart of utensils in the background. It turned out "Big Red" was a shot put champion back in college, and she was compelled to dust off her dormant skills on a blonde pervert who messed with the wrong Asian.

Tiny knew something that Joey didn't. There was no chance he was going to be allowed to win the following Saturday night. "Next week I fight Shamrock."

Joey considered his wrestling friend's cold hard fact, and was equally stumped.

Chapter 21

Guilt By Association

Mrs. Cassata watched with a mixture of pride and disgust as Scally shoveled her Sunday night feast into his mouth. Of course, she had not invited the little homewrecker, but it was hard not to appreciate someone so clearly enjoying her food. Finally, her indignation won, and she clicked her tongue.

Joey, knowing exactly what that meant, looked up from his plate. "What, Ma? He can't even eat over anymore? He's on the streets now."

"Don't get me started." She was about to take Scally's third serving away from him.

Joey picked up his friend's glass of clear liquid, spilling some in the process. "He's even drinking plain water."

"It's a little late for that." Even though Mrs. Cassata saw Scally fill his glass from the tap, she was convinced it was somehow still vodka.

"You guys say something?" Scally said, speaking around a mouthful of food. A piece of sausage dribbled onto his lip. Like a lizard, his tongue darted out and pulled the morsel back in.

Tired of playing mom to two would be grown ups, Mrs. Cassata just gave up. "No, you go right ahead."

The blonde with the bottomless stomach reattacked his plate with gusto. "This veal parm is killer, Mrs. C," he beamed, nearly choking on his words.

WRESTLING WITH JOEYLICIOUS

She simply shook her head. "You almost had me fooled, Robert. Going to meetings everyday – I thought you were turning yourself around."

"I'm still turnin'," the shameless phony tried to explain, taking a breather for the sake of digestion. "They say I'm really taking to those 15 steps."

Joey gave his idiot friend an elbow to the ribs. "There's only 12."

"I'm a special case. They added three more for me to hurdle." When it came to nonsense, at least Scally was quick on his feet.

"I don't doubt it," Mrs. Cassata muttered before accidentally knocking her cutting knife onto the floor.

Scally's eyes lit up like a Christmas tree. He knew this was his one chance to put a bow on his scrumptious free meal. If only Joey's mom would bend over to pick up that utensil in distress. But she wasn't budging. Did she even notice what had happened?

"You dropped your knife, Mrs. C." It was the least he could do.

Mrs. Cassata gazed at the schemer stoically. "I realize that."

"Aren't you going to pick it up?" Again: the least Scally could do.

"A gentleman might pick it up for me," she retorted.

"He might. He just might." Now he was just winging it.

Mrs. Cassata scoffed. "Waste." And then she bent over to retrieve her knife.

With cheetah like reflexes, Scally pulled out his flask from under his shirt, and poured the contents into his glass. The flask was replaced a split second before Mrs. Cassata straightened in her chair. Score! That would get his water up on its feet.

WRESTLING WITH JOEYLICIOUS

Joey watched the entire diabolical sequence seething in anger. But as bothered as he was by the blatant lack of respect toward his mother, he wasn't about to rat out his best bud. It was time to move onto the next pressing issue. "We're on top of the drinking, Ma. But we need your help with Father Randazzo, so Scally can at least get his job back."

"You'll get no help from me there," his mother said, finally putting her foot down. "He wants his job back, he can ask the good Father himself."

This was not the ideal response Joey had hoped for. "C'mon, Ma!"

"Better yet, the two of you can ask." She knew how to stick the metaphorical knife in when appropriate.

Even less ideal. "How did I get dragged into this?" Joey bemoaned.

Scally put down his suddenly empty glass of "water" and belched. "Guilt by association."

The wrestler glared at his easily breakable manager. "How would you like a flying elbow associated with your face?"

"Cool," Scally replied with a misunderstanding smile. "You need to practice a new move?"

* * * * *

Far earlier than he would have liked, Joey found himself sitting with Scally in Father Randazzo's office. It was so reminiscent of their time in school as misbehaving youths. The big difference being that the evil Sister Marie wasn't sitting across from them. That nun would make the other students quake in fear, but not these two. When Sr. Marie met Joey and Scally, she met her match.

Like that day in May of 1987, when the tag team delinquents

snuck out of school for an hour to score Madison Square Garden wrestling tickets. Hulk Hogan was defending his title against "King" Harley Race, and there was no way they were going to miss that. The Hulkster ended up winning, of course. But when Joey and Scally returned to school from the nearby shopping mall's Ticket Master, Sr. Marie was waiting for them. And she knew, somehow, that they had those tickets. And she was going to confiscate those tickets. It didn't happen. The two misdemeanor masterminds outfoxed her. Scally made up an excuse about a sick hamster he suddenly had to bring to the vet, and Joey had to come along for emotional support. "Gerry" the hamster was a lowly creature in God's kingdom, but Jesus cared especially for such lowly creatures so they were just doing the good Lord's work. What could a nun - even an evil one - say to that?

Back in the present with Fr. Randazzo now occupying Sr. Marie's chair, Joey held up his hands as if he were begging. "C'mon, Father, it's been weeks since that incident. Look how sorry he still is."

Scally picked at his nails as if he wasn't even a part of the conversation.

A frown flashed over Joey's face, but he still had to press on. "This whole episode has devastated him. He's devastated!"

His idle friend looked up with the sincere commitment of a wet fish. "Yeah."

Fr. Randazzo sniffed out the clear lack of emotion on Scally's part. "Not that I buy any of this, but I'll tell you what I'll do: Robert can have his job back, but-"

Scally didn't even wait for the priest to finish. "Awesome! So we're done here?" He got up, and was halfway to the door-

The priest held up a finger, "-but if he slips up just once more, he's gone for good." He pointed the finger at Joey. "And so are you."

Scally swayed his head as if he were listening to music. "Sounds fair." He casually plopped back down in his chair.

Joey shook his head in horror. "No, it's not fair! Father, whatta we in the mob now? I vouch for him, he screws up, and I take two in the back of the head?" He could swear he saw this play out in the director's cut of 1991's Mobsters. The great Richard Grieco surely met his demise in that very fashion.

"Yes, Joseph. That's exactly what I'm saying." Fr. Randazzo wasn't about to sugarcoat it.

At that, Joey stood up, ending the negotiations abruptly. He could never bet all his chips on Scally's hand. On a good day, his friend and manager was holding a two and a seven. "Scal, didn't you once say you could get your old job back at that bike shop?"

Chapter 22

"Life is a Ring"

If the body was one's temple, Joey's temple was showing more than a few cracks. But, on this day, he primarily arrived at the Men's Health Club to deal with another matter. Normally, he would never come to this particular place at this particular hour due to who would be at this particular place at this particular hour. But that was just the person he needed to see. So, as soon as he entered, he made a beeline to the envy of BRAWL who was in the middle of bench pressing.

"Shamrock, you got a sec?"

Shamrock didn't even acknowledge him. It wasn't the type of question worthy of interrupting his rep count.

"I need a favor," Joey said, pressing ahead with his mission. "Actually, it's a favor for Tiny."

At this, the Irish Adonis laughed as he continued to pump iron.

Joey was already beside himself. "What? I didn't even ask yet!"

Shamrock just kept right on laughing.

"Oh, you're such an dick," the Italian Dream shot back. Realizing this was a waste of time from the start, he stormed back toward the exit.

"Buddy, can you spot me over here?" a husky voice called out, interrupting Joey's departure.

Joey froze. He knew that voice from somewhere, but where?

WRESTLING WITH JOEYLICIOUS

When he turned to face the man who had addressed him, a familiar looking figure was rubbing his hands together clearly preparing to lift a tremendous amount of weight.

"Stone Cold?"

The pro wrestling legend and movie star "Stone Cold" Steve Austin grinned widely, and then lifted a can of beer as if offering a cheers to Joey for recognizing him.

The Italian Dream immediately started to hyperventilate. "Whatta you- How? Why?"

Holding up his hands, Joey's mammoth hero was quite used to this. "Calm yourself, Liscious." He approached his swooning fan with long strides that were just as intimidating as they were on TV.

Joey was about to pass out from the shock and excitement despite Stone Cold's words. The man had more championship belts than Joey had just plain belts.

Realizing the overwhelmed Italian wasn't improving, the Texas Rattlesnake stepped up his vocal soothing: "Deep breaths. C'mon."

Joey finally started to control his breathing as Stone Cold chugged his beer. "That'a boy," the world famous wrestler said approvingly. He patted Joey firmly on the back. "All better?"

"Uh, Stone, I don't think it's a good idea to be drinking while you're working out." Joey always knew how to properly break the ice.

"What?" This was already the beginning of one of Stone Cold's banter trade marks.

Thinking that he just wasn't heard, Joey went into more detail: "I said, I don't think you should be boozing while pumping iron. It's counterproductive."

"What?" the rippling figure repeated with more emphasis this time.

WRESTLING WITH JOEYLICIOUS

Again this was lost on the middle-aged wrestling upstart. "Is something wrong with your hearing? I just said-"

Frustrated, Stone Cold slammed his beer off Joey's head, sending him crashing into the leg press machine.

The mountain of a man then stood over the Italian Dream who was suddenly wide awake. "How do you let that Irish bastard get away with that crap?!"

Joey wiped the beer from his eyes as he shook off the unexpected blow. "I was being diplomatic for Tiny."

"Was I ever diplomatic when dealing with that sonofabitch, McMahon? You stop being a diplomat once you step into the ring." Stone Cold had a point. His long feud with the wrestling and business tycoon, Vince McMahon, was legendary. He once even attacked McMahon when he was laid up in the hospital, much like Mike Foley and his alter egos did to Joey even though that didn't actually happen.

Again: this was all lost on Joey. "But we're not in a ring, Stone."

"It's all a ring! Life is a ring!" The veins were now showing on the angry wrestler's neck.

Getting back to his feet, Joey marveled at the muscular man's philosophy. It all started to make sense. Finally. "That's pretty poetic. You come up with that yourself?"

Stone Cold shrugged with the modesty of a Buddhist monk. "I dabble."

Joey suddenly sensed a golden opportunity. "Can you help me help Tiny?" he asked, cutting right to the chase.

Not indicating whether he would or wouldn't, Stone Cold looked away and thought. "I like Tiny. He advised me on a stock once."

"So what do I do?" Joey was unfazed by his hero's good business sense.

WRESTLING WITH JOEYLICIOUS

Stone Cold's response was wordless but deafening. He pointed to the intimidating weight bar he was preparing to lift when he had called out to Joey in the first place.

Joey immediately objected, holding up his hands. "Stone, I can't lift my way outta this dilemma."

Stone Cold glared down at the suddenly puny Italian. "The hell you can't."

"Is this like a Mr. Miyagi thing?" Joey was really trying to play along, but he played at his own speed.

Done playing, the overpowering wrestler grabbed Joey and threw him down on the weight bench. "Lift," he commanded.

Quickly putting his hands under the bar that a professional body builder would struggle with, Joey finally gave in out of fear. "Okay, I'm lifting." But then his eyes darted nervously to the much bigger man. "You're spotting me, right? Cause I didn't even stretch yet."

This time Stone Cold's glare was not followed with words.

The silent gesture concerned Joey, but for the wrong reason. "You didn't hear a word I just said, did you? You should look into lip reading at least."

Completely deadpan, the not so deaf wrestler again dusted off his trademark. "What?"

Ignoring that for the time being, and suddenly filled with cockiness, Joey scoffed. "Then again I usually warm up with more weight than this. I don't even really need a spot-" Having talked himself into the mere formality, he lifted the bar but it predictably collapsed on his neck. Immediately. "Spotter," he called out sputtering. "Stone... help!.."

A pair of hands grabbed the bar, and lifted it off the desperately struggling bench presser.

Joey quickly sat up coughing for air. "Stone! Seriously?" But when he turned back for an explanation, he found himself

WRESTLING WITH JOEYLICIOUS

looking at a bemused Shamrock, not "Stone Cold" Steve Austin. As usual, the wrestling legend, just like all the others, was nowhere in sight.

Shamrock could only laugh as he headed off to the showers.

His Italian rival regained his bearings. "That's it, Shamrock," he shouted after him. "Our next match, it's on for real!"

* * * * *

Joey was rubbing the front of his semi-crushed neck as he exited the Men's Health Club. It was a harrowing experience sprinkled with the perfect balance of humiliation thanks to Shamrock's smug rescue. God, would he love to put his wrestling boot up that pompous ass's ass! He worked up more of a sweat just thinking about it than he did from his pitiful excuse of a workout. But just as he was being overwhelmed with thoughts of sweet revenge, Joey was rocked from his mental cloud when he inadvertently crashed into a passerby two steps from the gym. Incredibly, it was Anne-Marie.

For a moment, the two elementary school lovers just stared in disbelief at each other. Finally, they simultaneously spouted each other's name at equal volume.

Anne-Marie's reaction was far less welcoming than Joey's, however, as she added a disappointed "Again" after his name.

Joey looked from his long lost love to the gym, then back to Anne-Marie. "I didn't realize you were a member here."

"This is a men's gym," she responded coyly.

"Yeah, but uh... with all that gender neutral stuff going on now, I could probably get you in." Wardrobe and heroes aside, Joey liked to show that he was well-versed on all things current.

"No thanks." And if that didn't demonstrate her lack of

interest clearly, Anne-Marie then continued to walk in the direction she was originally heading: away from the gym.

Joey was prepared to follow her, but thankfully did not. "Maybe I can even show you a thing or two in the ring sometime," he called out instead.

Unfortunately, that got her to stop and turn back to him. She was not happy. "And then what? We team up, and take on old age homes together?"

He immediately realized he stepped in it. "Now, wait. That wasn't-"

"Do you know what happened after I brought my traumatized daughter back from your 'match' or whatever that was?" Anne-Marie pressed, not allowing her "ex" to get a word in edgewise. "We had to call my mother - her grandmother - six times just to make sure she was alright. My daughter was convinced she was in that fiasco. She has nightmares every night about some Mexican wrestler body slamming her Nana onto a Bingo table!"

"Puerto Rican." Joey's correction was tone deaf as usual.

"What?" she said, more than a bit flustered. Of course, she really didn't want him to repeat that.

"Una Grenada: he's Puerto Rican. But I'm pretty sure that wasn't your mother he tangled with- Wait, does she play Bingo?"

Anne-Marie also didn't need him to elaborate. "I have to get back to work," she simply said before attempting to escape again.

This time Joey started to follow her. The man-child just couldn't take a hint. "Oh, yeah. Your Rite Aid is just down the block- That's not why I picked this gym, though!"

With a heavy sigh, Anne-Marie knew that she would have to spell things out one painful syllable at a time.

WRESTLING WITH JOEYLICIOUS

Joey mistook this as a positive sign. "I was coming here since before I knew you worked there," he continued.

"Look, Joey: I realize we share fond memories," she started slowly. "You were the first boy I had a crush on, the first boy I kissed, the first boy I even let get to second base-"

"Technically, that was Scally," he interrupted, wanting to keep the record straight.

"It's 2020," Anne-Marie continued, ignoring the interruption and sharpening her diction. "I just don't think 'we' can work anymore. We're just different people now. You still live at home with your mom. I AM a mom!"

Joey thought of a middle ground. "Let me at least make things right with your daughter," he said with true contrition in his voice .

She folded her arms. "And how would you possibly do that?"

Sensing a crack in her armor, he had to think fast. "Uh... I could buy her an Elizabeth doll."

"I'm afraid to even ask what that is," she muttered with her eyes closed.

"She was the Macho Man's wife," Joey continued, stating the obvious.

Of course, this was not obvious to Anne-Marie, who simply stared blankly at him.

He did his best to elaborate, but at this point it was a lost cause. "You probably remember her as his manager. They got married later on."

"Goodbye, Joey." Finally, she left without turning back.

"I don't even have to buy Elizabeth," he desperately called out. "I have her in my room! I can get her now! She's still in the box; mint condition! Elizabeth goes for 60, 70 bucks easy in today's market! What's your daughter's name?! I can sign it for her!"

Chapter 23

With a Little Help to His Friends

Dirty and sweating profusely in the gym of Saint Dominick's elementary school, Lou Rossati and Una Grenada set up the ring for the upcoming Saturday night event. Didn't these guys get any help? Lou was about to keel over. Where was the crew? The love? The sense of community spirit? Apparently, it didn't exist. Joey entered to second that motion, because he wasn't there to lend a hand either.

Una Grenada glanced up before getting back to work. "Here to gloat, Lisch? I know I go down tomorrow, but no need to rub it in," he said offhandedly.

Joey, focused on his mission, politely ignored the Latin wrestler's rhetorical question. "Lou, I need a favor."

Lou didn't even look up. "And I need about 30 grand and a new prostate." He meant every word of that. He hadn't had a painless steady stream since the Iraq war. The first one.

"You gotta let me switch with Shamrock tomorrow," Joey continued.

"Your head bounce off the canvas one too many times? Shamrock fights Tiny."

Joey's head bounced off many things many times, but he had his noble reason. "I know."

"And you fight Tiny next week," Lou added.

"So just reverse it to this week. There's six wrestlers in this league. It's not like anyone at Saint Dom's is gonna know the difference."

Finally, Lou looked up with a purpose. "I'll know the difference! There's a certain level of integrity I'd like to maintain!"

A chuckle from Una Grenada reminded them that they weren't alone. "Are you feeling okay, Lou?"

The shady operator's mouth twitched. "Stay outta this, Grenada." His eyes bore into Joey. "Not to mention the posters I already printed."

Joey's ass may have been dumb, but he was no dumb ass, "You didn't pay for any posters, you cheap bastard!"

Another laugh at Lou's expense from Una Grenada came with another quip: "He's got you there."

Lou fumed at the Puerto Rican he sometimes confused for a Mexican. "I said, stay outta this!" Turning back to the Italian Dream, he tried to play off his anger. "What's all this about, anyway?"

"I told you. I wanna switch with Shamrock," Joey reiterated.

The little man's eyes narrowed. "Why?" He was no dummy either.

Instead of disclosing his heart to heart with Tiny, Joey searched for a metaphor that would best explain the situation. He found this: "Remember when Jesus fell the third time, and Simon came along to help carry the cross?"

Lou gave the suspect theologian an incredulous look before sticking a pin in his balloon parable. "You mean the same cross that Jesus would later be crucified on?"

"Well, yeah, but-" Joey knew he was already in trouble.

"Jesus hung out with a dude named Simon?" a perplexed Una Grenada asked, chiming in. "Is that where Simon Says comes from?"

WRESTLING WITH JOEYLICIOUS

Joey backpedaled further. "Maybe I'm not explaining myself right-" His metaphorical path was obviously not the straight and narrow.

At his wit's end, Lou pulled at the few hairs he had left. "Enough," he cried. "I'm getting a brain cramp! You switch with Shamrock tomorrow. Happy?"

Una Grenada's shoulders slumped. "So now I gotta fight that shanty Mick? Hate that guy, man!"

Joey gave his BRAWL companion a comforting smile. "I'll owe you one, alright?"

"Bet your ass you will," Una Grenada grumbled.

"Great," Lou cut in, looking between the two wrestlers. "Now can me and Grenada finish putting this ring together?"

Joey pursed his lips, knowing that he was about to press his luck. But he had to try. "I have one more favor to ask..."

* * * * *

Joey felt like he was walking on air as he hurried to Marine Park. The sun was down, so his search in the dark would be a bit more difficult. Still, homeless Scally was a predictable Scally, and Joey knew where all the comfortable benches were.

It didn't take him long to find a familiar looking figure curled up on the bench closest to the nearest liquor store. If there was any doubt about who it was, the burnt "Italian Dream" sheets covering the figure clarified the matter. Joey smiled as he ran over to his friend.

"Scal, wake up! I have great news!" Without waiting, he yanked his manager up into a sitting position.

Still in the middle of a pleasant dream, Scally's eyes were only half open. "Washi, where are you putting that? That

WRESTLING WITH JOEYLICIOUS

should go in Sayo."

"Wake up," Joey yelled as he gave the perverted Rip Van Winkle a good shake.

Scally finally stirred. "Huh?"

"Your ban has been partially lifted!" Joey's final gambit with Lou, although costly, had been effective. He would just have to do a little side work for the BRAWL wheeler and dealer - too shady to even get into for the purpose of this book.

Now fully awake, Scally's brain still had visions of Washi and Sayo. "Partially?"

"You still can't sit ringside or in the bleachers, but they're gonna let you run my memorabilia table from the lobby," his client explained fully. "Pretty neat, huh?!"

The manager wasn't impressed. "Says you."

"What's the matter?" Joey asked, suddenly concerned.

"That bike shop I used to work at ain't a bike shop anymore," the unusually dispirited blonde explained. "They use the place for pottery classes now."

Not seeing how that was relevant, Joey scoffed. "So you'll get another job."

Scally gave his friend a knowing look. "Funny you should say that. Weren't you just with me when I was offered another job?" He wasn't such a dummy either. Okay, he was, but still.

"When one Italian says to another what Father Randazzo said to me, you can't just jump in with both feet. You don't know how cold that water is." Really Joey? Again with the metaphors?

"He didn't mention anything about water, alright?!" Scally huffed, then laid back down on the bench, pulling the charred sheets over his head.

Joey watched for a moment. "At least you're sleeping okay," he lamented. But as he began to walk away, he didn't get far

~ 159 ~

before his desire to help his little friend outweighed self-preservation.

*****

The next afternoon, Joey and Scally stood just outside the Saint Thomas Aquinas Rectory. Joey picked up a handful of small rocks and examined them before finally choosing a nicely rounded one. Taking aim, he threw it at the second floor window. There was a ping as the rock bounced harmlessly off the glass.

Seconds later, Father Randazzo opened the window as Scally looked around for a way to contribute himself. The little menace found a much larger rock and launched it haphazardly just as the good priest stuck his head out.

Of course, Fr. Randazzo grabbed that same head in pain right after the hurling meteor bounced off it. "Ow!!!"

"Sorry, Father," Scally called out, less apologetically than he needed to.

The holy man who suddenly wasn't feeling so holy frowned down at his lost yellow sheep. "Robert, what the heck are you doing?!"

"I'm here to take back my old job," the lost sheep replied matter-of-factly.

Joey dropped the rest of his rocks. "Yeah, Father, I vouch for him. So he can start on Monday?"

The angry priest put both hands on the windowsill and squeezed. "He just hit me in the face with a rock! So he already screwed up again, and you know what that means!"

Joey held up his own hands. "Whoa, whoa, I vouched for him after you got hit! And you didn't even rehire him yet!"

Scally smiled at his friend's twisted but effective logic.

WRESTLING WITH JOEYLICIOUS

"Yeah, Father. You know... what he said."

Exasperated, Fr. Randazzo threw in the towel. "Fine! He starts again Monday! Now get outta here before I come to my senses! Both of you!"

"Thanks, Father," Scally responded with a wave.

The priest disappeared back inside the building.

Joey remembered something. "Wait, Father," he quickly called out. "I need a blessing for tonight's match!"

Something else occurred to Scally as well. "And can I sleep in the gym til my first paycheck?"

The only reply they got was the sound of the window slamming shut.

Scally interpreted the priest's reaction in a way only he could. "Wow," he said, turning to his pal who just vouched for him. "He's pissed at you."

Chapter 24
Too Sweat to be Sour

Memorabilia night! Tables for each wrestler's paraphernalia were set up in the lobby of St. Dominick's gym as scattered fans mulled about. Some bought, most just mulled. Scally, manning the Joeylicious table with his usual misguided exuberance, was covered from head to toe in "Bring the Violence" buttons. Other items for sale included "Italian Dream" pillows, "Man of the Hour" watches, "Tower of Power" towers, and a "Too Sweat to be Sour" cake. Joey approached dripping with excitement, visions of "$" signs dancing in his head. "Yeah, baby! That's what I'm talking about! We're gonna clean up tonight!"

Scally pulled his fist to his body like a cash register crank. "Cha-Ching!"

Noticing the scrumptious looking cake coated with green, white and red icing mimicking the Italian flag, Joey's smile widened. "Great, you remembered to pick up the 'Too Sweet to be Sour' cake! Thanks, Scal! You're the-" His expression changed for the worse as his eyes went over the cake again. His lips moved as he reread the chocolate lettered words on it. "Wait! 'Too Sweat to be Sour?'"

"Huh?" Scally looked at it from his position, not really able to read the cake upside down – not that he particularly cared either way.

"This cake says 'Sweat,'" Joey shouted, frowning at his so-called manager. "It's supposed to say 'Sweet!' 'Sweet!'" Yup, there it was in large, clear, chocolate font: S-W-E-A-T.

Sensing his client's mounting anger, Scally suddenly cared. "Uh... but you sweat a lot when you wrestle, so... so that makes you sour and tough to beat!"

Joey slammed his fist down on the table. "You idiot! Who wants to be sour?! I'm sweet!" After noticing one glaring mistake, he became critical of another matter. "And why the hell are you wearing all my buttons? It looks like you're wearing a 'Bring the Violence' suit! No one can see your Joeylicious sweatshirt with all that in the way!"

"The buttons are a new edition! I'm just tryin' to call attention to 'em!" Planning this night for months, this was to be the one piece of merchandise they were going to shove down everyone's throat. But Scally looked like target practice for a redneck with a BB gun.

"The buttons will sell themselves," the angry Italian countered. "You look ridiculous!"

That hurt his manager's feelings, and he looked away from his client/friend.

"You know what-," Joey muttered, throwing his hands in the air. "I don't have time for this. Thanks for helping. I gotta get ready."

Before Joey could get away, Scally wanted clarification on the disappointing turn of events. "Is it okay if I eat the cake?"

Joey half turned to make sure he heard that correctly. "What?" He did.

"You know, cause it's misspelled," Scally elaborated. Unfortunately.

"I don't-" Joey was just starting to prepare another argument, but decided it simply wasn't worth it. "Whatever," he relented with a heavy sigh. Then he just walked away. There were more pressing issues at stake than Scally eating the broken merchandise.

* * * * *

With the sounds of a small but rowdy crowd cheering and booing in the background, Joey gave Tiny a pep talk in the locker room. The big man was used to going down and staying down, so getting him pumped for the alternative should have been an easy sell. It wasn't. The closest Tiny ever came to victory was a near forfeit when Una Grenada got stuck in traffic on his way to the ring. The Italian Dream had to remind the human garbage disposal that no such traffic jams would be happening tonight. "Alright, Tiny, we're next! You ready to do this?!"

"I think so." Tiny was already uncertain.

Joey got in his face. "Whattaya mean, you think so?! Your boys are out there! It's their birthday! We gotta make this look good!"

Tiny bounced up and down in an effort to psych himself up. This almost caused an injury, an earthquake, or both. "Alright, alright, I'm ready!"

Joey slapped his wrestling companion on the back. "That's it! You're gonna kick ass like you've never kicked ass before!"

Forming fists, Tiny was ready to start pounding lockers. He couldn't remember the last time he was excited about a fight. Joeylicious would be his next meal, and his next meal would be vicious and delicious. "Let's do this," he yelled at the top of his lungs.

Joey began to worry. He was happy to create a monster, but he preferred a controllable one. A brief warning was in order: "Just don't lay on me for the tap out. I'm not looking to die out there tonight."

Tiny realized there was more to winning than just winning, but he wrinkled his forehead at Joey just the same. "How am I supposed to pin you?"

"Just put your foot on my chest. One foot with no pressure. It'll be like your signature pin move." Simple was also in order. The more Tiny had on his plate, the bigger the potential mess. Joey was not about to be mopped up off the canvas floor.

"Cool! I like it!" And, just like that, the pep talk had run its course.

As Joey nodded proudly, he was secretly praying inside. There was no way this would go as smoothly as planned. With nothing else to do about that, he smiled at his ecstatic opponent, and they both waited eagerly for their ring introductions.

* * * * *

Scally wolfed down a piece of the "Too Sweat to Be Sour" cake. Thanks to him and only him, it was already half gone. Other than a few "Bring the Violence" buttons that were now missing from his sweatshirt, no other Joeylicious items had been sold. Scally scanned the area and saw other tables selling their goods - especially, Shamrock's section which was almost wiped clean.

Hoping that maybe he had forgotten about some previous purchases, Scally opened a money container. Unfortunately, all he got was verification. There was nothing but two quarters inside.

* * * * *

WRESTLING WITH JOEYLICIOUS

The fight crowd was even smaller than anticipated. Apparently, the word of mouth marketing strategy that Lou had counted on following the "race war" between Gehrig's Ghost/Joeylicious and Milk Shake did not extend to St. Dominick's gym. New shady ideas would have to be thought of and fast. Otherwise, BRAWL would die a violent yet quiet death.

Speaking of quiet, as Joeylicious and Tiny fought in the ring, their voices could practically be heard over the audience. Was there another word for audience? If it wasn't for the two boisterous, miniature Tiny's hopping up and down in the front row of the bleachers, St. Dom's could've doubled as a speakeasy. It was the twin's first match, so they could care less about the crowd behind them; their old man was kicking ass in front of them.

Joeylicious fought back a smile as he caught sight of the twins and their enthusiasm. It hadn't been easy, but he had managed to make Tiny look like a champ. Deciding it was time to push the fight toward its conclusion, the Italian Dream bounced off the ropes and ran straight into the behemoth's flabby yet powerful arm - the perfect execution of a clothesline. Joeylicious crashed to the canvas, then sprang up right into a chop that Tiny had timed with the precision of a Swiss watch. Beaming, Tiny strutted around the ring, raising his arms triumphantly. He soaked up whatever cheers the crowd could muster as his twins gave each other a high five.

This time Joeylicious struggled to his feet for dramatic effect. Shaking off the damage, he snuck up on the premature celebrator and punched him in the back of his wrinkled, bald head. This was a big mistake, of course, because the backstabbing blow did nothing to hinder Tiny. Instead, it hurt Joeylicious's hand. For real. Well, some ice would take care of that later.

Tiny turned in anger and stomped on the Italian Dream's foot, causing Joeylicious to hop up and down in agony on his other foot. Tiny was too aggressive in his delivery, so again, Joeylicious was only half acting here. That life insurance policy he sold to BRAWL would've really came in handy about now.

Tiny, feeling his oats, then swung for the fences when he should've been focused on base hits up the middle. He actually attempted to kick Joeylicious in the chest. Predictably, the feeble attempt never reached its mark, and the big oaf lost his balance. As he fell hard to the canvas, the impact of his mass hitting the mat shook the entire ring (and the gym for that matter), taking Joeylicious down with him. For a moment, the two combatants just stared at each other, clueless on what to do next.

"Lisch, you gotta help me up," Tiny hissed, after trying to wobble to a sitting position at least.

Joeylicious wasn't ready to give the obese Ralph Macchio a pass. "Whatta you a karate expert all of a sudden?! What's with the kicking?!"

"I got cocky," Tiny responded with the appropriate amount of contrition.

Accepting the explanation, his friendly opponent relented. "Okay, I'll try and get you up, but it can't look like I'm helping."

"How you gonna do that?" Normally, this would take a room full of scientists to figure out, but there was no time. And the odds of finding a scientist out of this lot were slim to negative 46.

Joeylicious rolled over and tried to lift Tiny with an impromptu wrestling move that wasn't even remotely convincing. The audience picked up on this forgery immediately, and reigned down boos in kind.

The Italian Dream adjusted his grip to make things look more realistic. "Straighten up," he muttered. "Get your legs underneath you!"

"I can't," Tiny shouted, panicking.

Even though the disgruntled crowd was small, the objects they now hurled at the ring were not. Someone even managed to sling a stained toilet seat that missed Joeylicious's head by mere inches. Either someone had an incredible arm from the rest room, or someone took the seat with them to the bleachers. Both scenarios were equally horrifying.

Tiny looked over and saw the concern on his sons' faces.

Joeylicious continued to struggle. "I'll drag you to the ropes, so you can pull yourself up! Shove me aside when-"

All Tiny heard was the last bit, so he immediately shoved him halfway across the ring.

Joeylicious crawled back in pain. "Not yet," he whispered loudly. "Let me get you to the ropes first!"

"Okay, sorry!" Tiny was completely discombobulated, but he knew it was time to bear down.

With the crowd nearing total mutiny, Joeylicious finally managed to drag the mountain of mush to the corner of the ring.

Tiny responded by shoving his co-conspirator away again. Then he began to pull himself up using the ropes. He got his right arm around the first rung... followed by his left... then he got his right knee underneath him...

The crowd, picking up on the drama at play, began to cheer Tiny on. They were much more interested in this than the third rate fighting they had witnessed to that point.

Above the cheers, Tiny could hear his oldest twin boy:

WRESTLING WITH JOEYLICIOUS

"C'mon, dad! Get up!"

"You can do it," his other son added.

Keeping his emotions in check, the bald giant finished hauling himself up. With one final grunt and a pained grimace, he stomped his left foot down on the canvas and straightened with a roar.

The crowd erupted as if the New York Knicks had just won their first championship since 1973. Somehow another suspect toilet seat even went flying by. Even the ladies would have to pee standing up tonight.

Turning once again to his staged enemy, Tiny snarled. "Come get some, Lisch!"

With sweat pouring down his face, Joeylicious smiled before charging in. The big man delivered a double chop to the head, and the Italian Dream sank to the mat for a well deserved nap. Tiny was careful setting his one foot down on Joeylicious's chest, then he waited patiently for the ref to end the Good Samaritan's night to the count of three.

"Yes," the twins yelled, bursting into cheers. "Woo-hoo!" Their voices continued to echo over the rest of the crowd as their father and hero stomped around the ring victoriously.

Chapter 25

50 Cents?! What?!

The distant cheers had died down to a murmur, and Scally was still sitting at a fully stocked Joeylicious table. Of course, the cake was gone, but that would do little to lift his client's spirits once he bore witness to the sales travesty in the lobby. The scheming manager looked around with real concern as the remaining fans exited, and the other tables closed shop. What to do? What to do? Scally was starting to panic. Finally, with no other choice (at least in his mind), he grabbed the edges of the tablecloth and pulled them together into a large sack with all the Joeylicious items inside. Then he exited St. Dominick's running.

Outside, in the school parking lot, was a dumpster. Knowing that it wouldn't be long before Joey reemerged, Scally used his speedy momentum to sling the heavy sack into the open bin. Problem solved, he sprinted back toward the lobby, but stopped when the proverbial light bulb triggered. He looked down to see that he was still wearing the suit of "Bring the Violence" buttons. He hurried back to the dumpster, tore off the buttons and threw them away as well. Satisfied that he had completed his mindless task, Scally booked back to his master's table.

As soon he flopped down in exhaustion, a familiar voice greeted him from a distance: "You're kidding! We sold out?!"

Scally caught his breath, turned and fake smiled at his client.

WRESTLING WITH JOEYLICIOUS

"Yup."

Joey pumped a celebratory fist in the air. "I knew it! Awesome! A defeat well worth the humiliation! So where's the money? Hand it over."

Never one to carefully review all the details before setting a plan into motion (or any of the details for that matter), that was when Scally realized what he had forgotten. The word hit him over the head like an anvil. "Money?"

"Yeah, the money. It's in here?" Joey grabbed the money container sitting next to Scally's chair.

Scally leapt into action. "Don't open that," he yelped, stretching out his hand.

"Stone Cold" Steve Austin suddenly stepped up to the table, a Styrofoam cup of beer in hand. Of course, only Joey took notice of him. "Oh, you're not gonna like this, Liscious," he said, quick to ignite the chaos.

Joey's hero only confirmed his suspicion. He already knew Scally was hiding something. But when he opened the container to see the bad news for himself, he underestimated the depth of despair jingling inside: two quarters. Still. It took Joey a full minute to register his pitiful memorabilia earnings before he finally looked to his so-called manager with fire in his eyes. "What's this?"

Scally's face was a mask of dread.

"Someone's got some splainin' to do," Stone Cold added, stoking the brewing inferno.

* * * * *

Outside, a garbage truck was already backing up against the dumpster of Joeylicious items.

WRESTLING WITH JOEYLICIOUS

* * * * *

Inside, Joey was already snarling in Scally's face. "Where's the rest?"

Scally backpedaled. "Uh... we were robbed!"

"What?" Stone Cold said, busting out his trademark.

"Robbed?! You just said we sold out," Joey shouted, continuing his interrogation.

Caught between two lies, the blonde mastermind quickly tried to merge them. "Well, we sold most of the stuff! Then we were robbed, and they took the rest!"

"What?!"

Joey frowned at his hero: "Stone, you're not helping."

"Sorry, Lisch." Even imaginary heroes apologized.

Joey put his game face back on for Scally. "So how is that selling out?"

"It isn't exactly, but-" If Scally backpedaled anymore, he would be getting squashed against Lou's office wall again.

"This guy's acting drunker than me, and I took all his drink tickets," Stone Cold said, unable to resist chiming in. He emphasized his point by chugging his beer, crumpling the Styrofoam cup and tossing it.

Joey continued to glare at his friend. "Scally, if you pocketed my earnings, I will find out!"

This was the moment Stone Cold was waiting for. "Hit him already! Remember, life is a ring; no time for diplomacy!"

* * * * *

Outside, a garbage man exited the garbage truck and attached a steel cable to the Joeylicious dumpster.

WRESTLING WITH JOEYLICIOUS

* * * * *

Inside, Stone Cold was getting giddy. "Turn him upside down, and shake the little sonofabitch!"

Near panic, Scally was practically ducking from his client now. "They had weapons and ski masks!"

"What?" Stone Cold asked yet again, cracking his knuckles.

Joey was about ready to make his wrestling legend proud. "The robbers?! How come no one else saw anything?! Where are the cops?!"

"Uh... everyone was busy with their tables," Scally blabbered. "It was chaos out here!"

Stone Cold's next "What?" had a musical quality to it. He had fully established the rhythm of his trademark.

"Why didn't you call the cops?" Joey pressed further, hoping that his deviant manager would finally admit the truth.

Although Stone Cold was eager for fists to start flying, he was quite content with Joey's verbal lashing. For now. "Let's see him crawl out of that logic box."

Looking around, Scally tried to stall for time. If he could just come up with the proper bullshit, his Joeylicious universe would be back in balance. "Wait, wait, I think..." He closed his eyes as if he was suddenly in a trance.

Perplexed, Joey looked to Stone Cold before turning back to Scally. "What?! What is it?"

Scally held out a hand. "I'm seeing a dumpster..."

"What?" Joey and Stone Cold responded in unison. They were equally surprised by their perfect timing.

"That's my line, Lisch," Stone Cold griped.

Sensing his client's confusion, Scally regained his footing. "I said, a dumpster," he shouted, pressing forward with his ruse. "Did Tiny box your ears in the ring?"

WRESTLING WITH JOEYLICIOUS

* * * * *

Outside, the steel cable lifted and tilted the dumpster, emptying the Joeylicious contents into the garbage truck.

* * * * *

Inside, Joey lifted and tilted a suspicious eyebrow. "A dumpster?"

"A black one- No, green!" Scally was scrambling again.

Stone Cold's patience was waning if it hadn't waned already. "Now he's just playing with you. He must be drunk. If you don't hit him soon, I will."

"Stone, I got this," Joey yelled, holding up a frustrated hand. Then he refocused on Scally. "What the hell are you talking about?!"

Finally, something other than Joey's ire caught Scally's attention. "Stone? Who's Stone," he asked, welcoming the distraction but honestly confused.

Stone Cold was still ready to pounce. "I don't think you have this, Liscious."

Joey grabbed his manager by the collar. "Scally!"

The blonde menace snapped to. He knew his farce was losing steam. "The Psychic Hotline: remember you told me I should work there?"

"No, I didn't!" And Joey was already beside himself.

Stone Cold scoffed. "That's it! I'm stunning him!" He got into position for his signature wrestling finisher.

"I'm gifted," Scally pleaded. "They had me in that special class!"

"Yeah, Special Ed," Joey retorted.

~ 174 ~

WRESTLING WITH JOEYLICIOUS

Stone Cold laughed. "Ha! Good one! Get him, Lisch! Don't take any crap from this lush!" For an imaginary being, he was really eating this up.

Scally suddenly straightened. "C'mon, hurry! I know where your stuff is!" He ran outside, and made a beeline for the dumpster.

Of course, Joey didn't believe the blatant lie, but he wasn't about to let the imp escape from his well deserved beating.

Stone Cold shrugged, then sauntered after both of them.

Scally reached the dumpster just as the garbage truck turned out of the parking lot, and drove off. He completely missed the significance of this as Joey caught up to him and glared.

"Well?" his more than suspicious client asked.

Scally looked into the dumpster, and saw that it was empty. His mind raced. "Uh... maybe it's in a different dumpster."

An unseen but nearby Stone Cold had a metallic echo to his signature question: "What?!"

Joey was done with the charade. "No, I think this is the dumpster right here."

"The jig is up, little pup!" Again there was a metallic echo to Stone Cold's unseen words.

Joey closed in on his puny manager. "And you're going in for a closer look!"

"Wait, Joe-" Scally was lifted into the air. "No, don't," he screeched, continuing to protest.

Joey body slammed the blonde idiot into the dumpster just as Stone Cold popped up from inside it. The wrestling legend beamed and held up a hand. "Hell yeah, Liscious!"

Joey gave his hero a high five.

Stone Cold nodded approvingly. "It's about time you handled an Irishman properly!" He tossed Joey a can of beer, and signaled that it was time for a toast by lifting his own beverage.

Joey opened his beer with a huge smile, but a thought struck him before he could celebrate with his new friend. "Wait, Stone- Why are you in a dumpster?"

"What?" Stone Cold responded. Of course, this was the one word that should've immediately given Joey pause.

Nope. "I heard things get rough when you guys retire, but-"

"Whatt?!11" That didn't sit well with "Stone Cold" Steve Austin.

Still clueless to the rippling figure's usage of the word, Joey thought he would conclude the evening with a thoughtful recommendation: "I really think you need to have a doctor check on those ears."

Stone Cold grabbed Joey, and performed his signature stunner on him. Then he stuffed him into the dumpster on top of Scally.

"Hey!" An unseen metallic echo rang out once more. But this time it came from a scrawny someone who didn't appreciate reigning Italians.

Strutting away from the dumpster, the wrestling legend couldn't help but to cap off the evening his way: "And that's the bottom line, because Stone Cold said so!" He certainly did.

Chapter 26

No Time to Pack!

Scally, scuffed up and dirty with a rotten banana peel stuck to his Joeylicious sweatshirt, schemed for an angle as he looked up at the front door of his parents' house. This would be a tough sell. His ability to talk himself into and out of trouble usually worked about half the time. Okay, a quarter of the time. Okay, hardly ever. But these current odds fell somewhere between hardly ever and never. His mother and father knew the tricks of his suspect trade as much as anyone, and living without him these past few weeks must have felt like a second honeymoon.

Finally, the prodigal son shook off any misgivings, and moseyed up the porch steps with a slight limp. He would return home on his own terms - the only terms he ever knew.

He rapped on the door loud enough for half the neighborhood to hear, and his father soon answered. Understandably, the older Scally was not happy. This late night visitor was not just visiting. And he knew it.

Scally smiled devilishly as if he had an offer for a struggling soul. "Hey, Pop. Mind if I crash the night?"

Mr. Scally's look of annoyance turned to disgust. "You're a mess."

"And maybe a few after that." Scally noticed the banana peel hanging off him, and tossed it aside.

It was clear the older Scally wasn't interested in the bartering terms his son was fishing for. "I believe we had an arrangement," he reminded him coldly.

"What arrangement was that?" the blonde time bomb asked as innocently as a wolf in wolf's clothing.

"You not living here-" Mr. Scally choked on his words as the stench of his son finally reached his nose. Taking a step back, he looked like he was about to gag. "What is that smell?! Were you rolling around in garbage?" Apparently, the banana peel wasn't an obvious enough clue.

"Funny you should say that. But I am sober." Scally knew what his father wanted to hear.

The overwhelming odor of dumpster remnants masked any possible whiff of alcohol, but Mr. Scally wasn't about to take his son at his word. He stepped forward, blocking the doorway. "Says who?"

"Says me standin' upright." Almost as an afterthought, he threw in something else he knew his father would want to hear: "And I have a job."

"Yeah. In wrestling management." The emphasis on those last two words made it clear the older man was not sold on this news either.

"I'm workin' for my old school now," Scally clarified, stepping up his game with, of all things, the truth.

"Doing what?" Mr. Scally responded with equal but curious skepticism.

"What's it to you?!" Didn't his father know that short, direct answers meant that, at worst, he was only lying slightly? When he wanted to truly sell an invented story, he would always say far too much. Scally folded his arms as he watched the figure blocking the door analyze the data. "So can I come in, or not?" he pressed.

"I have a feeling I'm going to regret this." And with a heavy sigh, Mr. Scally stepped out of the way.

"Oh, I think it's more than a feelin'." Scally chuckled deviously as he slipped by his old man, and stepped into his old home. Tonight his visions of Washi and Sayo sugarplums would dance in his own childhood twin bed.

* * * * *

Joey was spread out on his own childhood twin bed with his feet dangling in the air as he mindlessly surfed the internet. Still in his sweaty wrestling outfit, he suffered from post-match depression. It was one thing to lose, even for a good cause, but this week he lost everything. Including the sale of two "Bring the Violence" buttons, he made a lousy $48.00 before expenses. If he included his entire memorabilia table, minus the two buttons, as an expense (which he did), he was buried in red ink. And now he would have to wait another whole week to feel the adrenaline from the 10 escaped convicts that would most likely double as fans at the next BRAWL event.

Something on Joey's laptop caught his eye, and all those negative thoughts suddenly washed away. He bolted up, his eyes almost popping out of his head. He quickly re-read, then re-re-read, then re-re-re-read the web page to make sure he wasn't hallucinating.

"Holy crap!" He stared at the advertisement for an upcoming Hulk Hogan autograph signing at the Hulkster's brand new beach shop in Tampa, Florida. "When?! When?!"

Joey's fingers moved faster than his brain as he scrolled down for more details. The ad took him to a page with the information he needed, and the excitement was boiling over. That is until he read, re-read, and re-re-read the date of the signing. "Tomorrow?! Damn!"

Scowling at the screen, he wasn't ready to give up so easily. He pulled up a calendar, a map, and a calculator. After quickly running the numbers, he clenched his fist in victory. "I can make it!" Far more forcefully than necessary, he then slammed the laptop shut, and grabbed some traveling items. "Ma," he called out to the other bedroom. "Can I borrow the car to meet the Hulkster in Tampa?"

"Florida?" As usual, her distant voice was full of skepticism.

"I'll leave tonight to beat the traffic." Of course, his sketchy math hadn't considered tomorrow's traffic. At best, it was a 17 hour drive from Brooklyn to Tampa.

"What about Sunday mass?! Father Randazzo is reenacting the Sermon on the Mount in full garb tomorrow." This was the beginning of the argument Joey had expected from his mother, but something about that vexed him.

With a wrinkled forehead, he looked at the wall her voice came from. "Again?!" He knew the good priest was committed to his work, but where was he getting the scratch for all the wine and fishes. Didn't imaginary Ric Flair discuss this with him recently?

"Just promise me the drunk isn't going with you," Mrs. Cassata said, basically caving with one sticking point.

Joey frowned. "Ma, he's my manager!"

"Not in my car he isn't," she yelled, putting her foot down.

Joey thought about what had just transpired between him and his so-called manager, and realized there would still be lingering bad blood.

He looked at the nearest clock: 11:30 PM.

Plus, even if he was allowed to pickup Scally, there wasn't enough time. If it was a choice between taking his friend, who had essentially stolen from him, or not leaving to meet his hero

~ 180 ~

WRESTLING WITH JOEYLICIOUS

at all, Joey knew where his allegiance lied.

* * * * *

Four and a half minutes later, still in his soiled wrestling outfit, Joey was on his way to Tampa, Florida. His mother's 2007 Honda Civic didn't have much head or leg room, or kick for that matter, but he would've taken a tricycle to meet the golden giant at the end of the Highway 95 rainbow. Unable to keep the excitement to himself, and ignoring all thoughts of misguided guilt, he called the one man who would understand his delirium fully - the same man he left behind. "Scal, you're never gonna believe it! I'm on my way to meet the Hulkster!"

On the other end of the line, Scally had already made himself comfortable in his parents' living room. Decked out in boxers along with his customary tank top/wife beater, he was focused, not on Joey's extraordinary words, but on the toy Lego Fort sitting on the coffee table in front of him. He was obviously still salty over a recent event. "I just took a four minute shower, and still stink. That's the last time you throw me out with the trash!"

"Forget that! I just said-"

"Joe, you're just havin' another episode! These wrestling heroes are all in your head!" For all Scally knew, his friend was crying wolf. His condition was detrimental before, but crippling of late.

"But this is different," Joey insisted.

"One sec." Scally lowered his cell as a shadow moved over his fort. He looked up to find his stern father looking down at him. "Pop, can't you see I'm busy here?"

"Your mother and I were talking-"

"Good for you and Ma. Keep talkin'." Scally refocused on

his friend's vivid imagination. "So Joe-"

"If you're going to live under this roof, you need to start paying rent," Mr. Scally persisted.

That got his son's attention. "On my assistant gym teacher salary?! I might as well have the school forward my checks right to you and Ma!" Not a bad idea actually. That would at least put a dent in his outstanding neighborhood bar tabs.

"Son, listen-"

"I'll tell ya what, though," Scally pointed at the precarious fort that looked like a poor man's rendition of the picture on the Lego box, "I'm workin' on my architectural career. Once the big bucks start rollin' in on this front, you and Ma will be sorted."

It was too late in the evening for Mr. Scally to be dealing with his son now anyway. After a sigh, the shadow cleared.

Scally paid little mind to his father's latest defeat, and again refocused. "Sorry, Joe."

Joey cut ahead of a car in the fast lane. It wasn't moving all that slowly; he just had the Civic humming. "Listen: I'm meeting Hogan at his beach shop in Tampa. He's signing autographs there tomorrow afternoon!"

That already sounded more legitimate than Joey's usual ramblings. Scally could also hear the sounds of the road over the phone. He sprang up off the couch certain his friend was heading his way. "What?! No way!" He was halfway to the stairs in a nanosecond. "I'll be ready in five!"

Instead of offering his manager a soft landing, Joey just tore off the band-aid: "Sorry, Scal. No time. If I drive through the night doing 90, I just might make it!"

Scally stopped dead in his tracks. Blinking uncontrollably, he couldn't believe what he just heard. "So why are you callin' me then?!"

"For moral support?" Realizing the call was a mistake, it was the best Joey could muster.

"Tease!" Without warning, Scally hung up on his so-called friend, and stormed off to his room. It was either that, or back to the Lego fort with the threat of his father restarting the rent conversation. Maybe he would at least find solace with Washi and Sayo waiting for him in his dreams.

Joey looked at his cell as if that couldn't have been helped. Shaking it off, he remembered that he had everything he needed and smiled. He popped the CD of the Rocky III soundtrack into the car stereo, and rocked out to what else but "Eye of the Tiger" by Survivor. Life was good for the Italian Dream, and it was about to get better.

"Yeah! That's what I'm talking about, brother," a second voice suddenly echoed through the vehicle much to Joey's delight. "My film debut!" Sitting shotgun was the man, the myth and legend the struggling wrestler was actually on his way to see in the flesh: Hulk Hogan.

Joey turned the music down a hair.

"Although, I did toss Stallone around the ring like a little bitch in my scene," the blonde giant continued.

"Hulkster, it was a draw," Joey countered. He was never shy to correct his heroes even when his heroes didn't need correcting.

"Are you kidding me?! That was some Hollywood B.S. if there ever was!" Thankfully for Joey, Hogan was more amused than angry at his risky reminder.

"Dramatic license," Joey said. Each attempted correction was like another toe being dipped into the pool of danger.

"Thuderlips does not fit into the jurisdiction of dramatic license. I was the ultimate male, against the ultimate meatball!" Not even Joey could argue with that.

And he didn't. "At least you were both ultimate," he said, finally pointing out a positive.

Hogan conceded with a half-hearted shrug. "Good song, though." He cranked the stereo to the max, and the pair sang along gleefully for the next few miles.

Chapter 27
Enter Sandman

Five hours later, with the thrill of Joey and Hogan's "Eye of the Tiger" duet long in the rearview mirror, undeniable sleep was elbowing its way into the still moving car. Joey hadn't pulled an all-nighter since he got his gym teaching job, and the furthest he had ever driven from Brooklyn was to New Jersey.

Wrestlemania 29 was at Metlife stadium back in 2013, and he and Scally had managed to score tickets to see John Cena defeat the Rock for the title. His mother had allowed his best friend and manager to ride along in the Civic then, but predictably, there were bumps in the road; the biggest coming when Scally threw his beer at a limo that tried to pass them in a gridlock. Incredibly, Judge Ito from the infamous O.J. Simpson trial was a passenger in the limo. When the beer smashed against his window, he rolled it down and berated the two Brooklynites, threatening them both with jail. If the traffic hadn't loosened up, and the celebrity judge hadn't been a wrestling fan, they probably would have spent that night in the clink. And now the mere memory of that was about to carry the Italian Dream off to a deep sleep. He shook it off with a wide yawn, and rubbed his teary eyes.

The sound of snoring drew Joey's attention to the passenger riding shotgun, and he gave his hero a disapproving look. Hulk Hogan was failing to help his "pradagi" complete his trip to see... well, Hulk Hogan. It suddenly dawned on the "pradagi" that if the Hulkster was asleep, he could at least make a more personal call. Quietly, he did just that.

In her bedroom, Anne-Marie was jolted awake by the sound of her cell vibrating on her night stand. Initially, she tried to hit the snooze button on her alarm clock before realizing it was her phone making the silent racket. Rubbing her eyes, she verified the time.

It was 4:34 AM.

Flopping back down in bed, she put the cell to her ear. "Whoever this is: unless someone died, you are about to," she said with her eyes closed.

Joey kicked off the conversation by missing the tee by a foot and a half: "Anne-Marie, did I wake you?"

That answered that question. Anne-Marie only knew one person who could be so oblivious. "No, Joey. I've been up milking the cows for at least an hour," she responded in kind. "How did you get this number?"

Joey read sarcasm like a blind bulldog read braille. "You're in the book. Didn't you get the Elizabeth doll I left on your porch? I knocked a few dozen times, but no one answered."

"Right, the doll - for Veronica..." Her eyes drifted to the female wrestling doll, still in the box, sitting on her dresser. It was a neat gift even though her precocious daughter cared little for dolls and less for wrestling. As annoyed as she was by the early wake up call, Anne-Marie couldn't help but smile at her childhood sweetheart's kind gesture. "That was very nice of you."

"Is that your daughter's name? She must be a princess." He was sucking up to his old flame, of course. But what choice did he have at 4:34 AM?

"Yes, Veronica. And she is." Her smile faded as sleep tried to pull her back in. "Listen, Joey: it's four-thirty in the morning. Can we-"

"I know, I'm sorry," Joey said, practically completing Anne-Marie's sentence for her. There was actual sincerity in his voice. "I just needed someone to help me stay awake while I drove, and you were the first person I thought of."

Staring up at the ceiling, his long ago ex started to soften. "Where are you going in the middle of the night?"

"I have to make it to Tampa by the afternoon to see the Hulkster!" As much as he wanted to, there was no way to say that calmly.

Briefly forgetting that she completed grammar school long ago, Anne-Marie suddenly shot up in bed. "Hulk Hogan?! He was always your favorite. I can't believe you haven't changed at all since the eighth grade."

"You know me! I've had the same hair cut since before then even." Well, at least he added the blonde highlights. "When I find something I like, I stick with it."

A sense of nostalgia washed over Anne-Marie as she thought of Joey as a kid. For all his faults, he always had a big heart. "It's nice to see that when Joey loves something, he loves it forever." She didn't realize the gravity of her response until she said it.

Joey's follow-up should have been a layup. "Exactly! Like my Ma and the Hulkster!" It wasn't.

Again her smile faded. "Oh... I was thinking... Never mind." Yanked back into the present, something else struck her curiosity. "Wait, are you driving to Florida all through the night by yourself?"

Joey's eyes moved to his traveling companion. "Not exactly. My shotgun is currently out cold, snoring up a storm."

Ann-Marie nodded, knowing exactly what he meant – or at least she thought she did. "Scally could always fall asleep anywhere. I don't hear him snoring though-"

Joey immediately realized his slip of the tongue. "No, not Scal-" His brain scrambled to catch up. If he mentioned the Hulkster was with him on his way to meet the Hulkster, the future Mrs. Cassata would immediately hang up and seek witness protection. Thankfully, he recovered just in time. "Yeah, Scal's the worst! Remember the time he fell asleep in Miss Whalen's class and had a wet dream?"

Anne-Marie laughed. "How could I forget! He told everyone he dropped Elmer's glue on his lap. So gross!"

Joey sighed with relief. "We really had some fun times back then, didn't we? Hey, let me take you and Veronica out for ice cream when I get back." When Anne-Marie didn't respond right way, he was suddenly concerned again. Was she really going to turn him down? Or had she fallen asleep again? "Hello?.. Ann-Marie, are you still there?"

She pursed her lips, and looked out the window. "Uh, okay, Joey. Why not? That should be fun. Just call me first, okay?"

Joey was ecstatic. "I'm calling you now," he said, letting his mouth get ahead of his brain again.

"I mean, when you get back: call me then." Was she already having second thoughts?

"Okay, great! Same number?" And would that give her third thoughts?

Anne-Marie just hung up, and was fast asleep before her head hit the pillow. Whether or not she heard Joey's final stroke of genius was anyone's guess.

The Casanova in the Civic was left perplexed. "Anne-Marie?" He looked at his cell. Realizing she must have hung up, he grinned refusing to take that as a bad sign. "I guess it's a date then." Now he had something else to look forward to. Was this the rollicking beginning to the greatest day of Joey's

WRESTLING WITH JOEYLICIOUS

life? "Sweet!" He certainly thought so.

* * * * *

But with the sun up just a few hours later, the end of Joey's greatest day, and of his life, was suddenly a real possibility. He was fast asleep in the driver's seat with his foot still pressed firmly on the gas. He and Hogan snored together like a musical counterpoint straight from the unreleased archives of Johann Sebastian Bach. They drifted over to the side of the highway, the ride becoming much bumpier as the Civic began to scrape the shoulder.

Hogan stirred first, his drowsiness quickly giving way to the realization of the danger at play. "Wake up," he screamed, directly into Joey's ear.

If that had come from the real Hulkster, Joey would have woken with tinnitus. Instead, he just woke. Somehow.

Hogan grabbed the wheel, and steadied the Civic a split second from total disaster. Crisis averted, the blonde giant then glared at the unintentional Italian kamikaze.

Playing the incident off as no big deal, Joey tried to clear his throat. "Did you sleep well?" But his voice betrayed him. He sounded like a female hyena in heat.

As if by magic, Hogan did an emotional 180 and shrugged casually. "Not bad actually. You?"

"Well-"

Before Joey could finish his thought, Hogan grabbed the back of his head and slammed it against the steering wheel.

Joey sat up and tried to regain his bearings.

"Now pull over," his wrestling mentor ordered. "You're getting some coffee!"

"Breakfast, too?" Joey hadn't planned on eating anything

during the trip except for the half melted Zagnut bar he packed in haste.

Hogan did the math. "Why not? I don't usually show up at my signings til three."

Chapter 28

The Vegan Who Wasn't There

Scally stood at the refreshment table of his next sex addiction meeting scarfing down a plate of donuts. He had hoped to pick up where he left off with Washi and Sayo, but his hopes were soon to be dashed when the "all business" counselor was the next to arrive.

"Good morning, Scally."

"Hey, buddy. What's shakin'?" Scally asked as much as stated before shoveling in another donut.

"We should talk," the counselor said, cutting right to the chase. His tone was ominous.

"When don't we? That's why I'm here." Scally was too busy deciding which donut he would devour next to pick up on any negative vibes.

"There's been some complaints by other members of the group," the counselor continued.

"What kind'a complaints?" The hungry imp was still hardly interested.

"Two kinds, actually. Well, one kind by two members."

Scally gave the donut he was currently destroying a guilty look before finally turning his full attention to the counselor. "Is this about me takin' too many donuts?"

"No. Although, that has been brought up by other members - just not the two we're currently discussing." This was true. In fact, one angry sex addict, who often baked for the group, had to be restrained at the previous meeting when Scally snuck out early with an entire batch of vanilla frosted cupcakes.

"So spit it out. The sexual healing is about to begin." With that, the scrawny blonde with the sweet tooth polished off yet another tasty treat.

"That's just it. There won't be any more of that for you here," the counselor stated plainly, fed up with the one-man donut eating contest. "At least not the sexual healing you're supposed to be getting. We took a group vote... you've been exiled."

Scally was shocked and appalled, even if it wasn't in that order. But before he could muster a flimsy defense, his two angels of the Orient walked in. They both noticed the "rapid firing sex machine" immediately, and then turned away from him in shame. Scally read his final verdict in large bold print.

With nothing left to say, he snatched one last glazed donut and stormed out of the room. He knew where he wasn't wanted, which was pretty much everywhere, but this time he had his principals.

"Scally, wait up," Sayo called out just as he was exiting the facility.

He stopped and turned, "reluctantly" giving the Asian addicts time to catch up.

Sayo's guilt was written all over her face. "We're sorry we got you thrown out. It's just that..."

"We're sexually frustrated," Washi cut in less apologetically.

"And have been - ever since we broke up with our boyfriend," Sayo added with a nod.

Scally looked between the two beautiful enigmas with a furred brow. "Our boyfriend? I mean, your boyfriend? Both of you?"

Sayo smiled sensually. "We like to share."

"Just not with a psycho, samurai stalker like our ex is,"

WRESTLING WITH JOEYLICIOUS

Washi elaborated.

Clearly, the conversation had taken an unexpected turn. But was it for the better, or worse? The cautious blonde still wasn't sold either way. "Samurai? As in the sword?"

Sayo looked to her friend. "That's why we couldn't take you to our place! He's always watching us there."

"So when you got us all worked up...," Washi continued.

"...and things didn't work out at your roommate's mother's apartment...," Sayo added.

"We lashed out," Washi concluded.

Sword wielding ex in the picture or not, Scally nodded understandingly. "I see."

Sayo touched his arm. "But we wanna make it up to you!"

Washi seconded the motion by touching his other arm. "Yeah, Scally. I can't believe I'm saying this, but could you ever forgive us?"

Scally's insides were about to burst. "I don't know. What kind'a penance did you have in mind?" he asked with a squeak in his voice.

Both women gave him a devious smile.

* * * * *

Sitting in the booth of a truck stop diner, Joey savored every aroma that emanated from the French toast and bacon in front of him. Hulk Hogan sat across the table with an omelet and hash browns. He savored neither. Both men also had a cup of coffee to go with their food. As Joey dug in with the fervor of a Buffalo bison, the Hulkster just sat their stoically - his breakfast and coffee untouched.

"Brother, why did you order this for me?" Hogan asked, truly perplexed.

"It would be rude of me to eat alone, wouldn't it?" Joey said matter-of-factly.

"You should be on a strict budget for this trip." Between this and his Rite Aid hair dye comments, maybe the wrestling legend really was an accountant on the side.

"I have some cash left." Joey responded with a mouthful, reassuring his mentor.

Hogan, much like Mrs. Cassata, gave the Italian Daydream a concerned look. "You do realize I'm not really here, right?"

"I know that," Joey muttered into his plate, lacking conviction.

"On top of which, I'm a vegan now. So I couldn't eat this anyway."

Joey stopped chewing. This was news to him. Being from South Brooklyn, he couldn't exactly relate. But he could criticise that puzzling statement constructively: "Hulkster, there's no meat in that."

"An omelet is dairy," the healthy blonde giant replied, annoyed that he had to point that out. "Plus, there's cheese in it."

"I have no idea what you're saying to me right now." Having slept through most of the 21st century, Joey clearly mistook "vegan" for just a muscular vegetarian.

"Never mind." Hogan could only shake his head as the waitress arrived with a kind smile.

"Is everything alright over here?"

"Yeah, we're fine." Joey forgot that there was no "we" in "a man eating alone at a truck stop diner."

The waitress's smile wavered as she looked over at the untouched omelet sitting on the empty side of the table. "Expecting someone?" she asked, reaching for the most likely explanation.

WRESTLING WITH JOEYLICIOUS

Joey looked up at her with a wrinkled forehead, then at Hogan's food with an equally wrinkled forehead, then back at her - forehead unchanged. "No, why do you ask?"

Not the explanation she had hoped for, so the waitress opened door number two: "Would you like me to wrap the omelet?"

"What's with all the questions? I just told you everything is fine!" He took a swig of coffee. Surely the prying intruder would be gone by the time the cup left his lips.

Still unclear as to what was actually happening, the waitress decided that she wasn't paid enough to figure it out. She left the hungry man with the black wrestling singlet and red boa to himself.

Hogan watched her leave. "Brother, she's just doing her job. She probably thinks you're talking to a ghost."

"But you're not a ghost. The real you is still alive." Joey had clearly thought this through.

"Have you ever imagined a dead wrestling legend?" Hogan asked curiously.

"Not that I recall..." Joey was just as curious.

"I wonder if that would be considered a ghost if you did." The rippling figment of Joey's imagination was doing a deep dive into his own imagination. The mind boggled.

"Wait, I did actually," the hallucinating Italian suddenly remembering. "Piper!"

Hogan couldn't help but roll his eyes. "Oh, that bastard."

Joey took immediate offense. "Hey! Respect!"

The Hulkster didn't feel the need to apologize. "I respected the man. But he was a nemesis, so he's still a bastard. I'm sure he calls me much worse from wherever he is now."

Joey couldn't find fault in that logic. "Interesting point." Then he did a deep dive into his own imagination, which was also Hogan's imagination - or Hogan's was his. Is anyone still following this? "Do you think the real you knows this conversation is actually happening?"

"No." There was no hesitation in Hogan's response.

Joey wasn't satisfied. "'No,' you're not sure, or 'no,' you don't think the real you knows?"

"The latter." Hogan clarified.

Joey frowned at the tattered remains of his French toast. "How can you be so sure?"

"Because the real me has a life," his hero responded. Maybe that was cruel, but it was definitely hilarious.

Chapter 29

100 Miles to Hulkster Heaven

Scally returned to his parents' house at around noon, and found it as quiet as a mime's funeral. This was a good sign. If his parents were gone, round two with Washi and Sayo would end in a knockout, or a standing eight count, or a TKO, or a decision in his favor, or a disqualification in his favor, or a draw - he wasn't picky. Bottom line: it would be a mind, body and spirit altering experience on the plus side.

At that moment, Scally thought of his mother, and felt soiled somehow. Where the heck had she been? He hadn't seen her since he moved back in straight from the dumpster. His father had that "thousand yard stare" of a hitman of late. Did he murder his mother after he was exiled to the Cassata's, and bury her in the wall? Or was his mother just out shopping? Who could tell?

Feeling the urge to wet his whistle, Scally strolled into the kitchen and found his father sitting alone in silence, staring into nothingness. It was like he was suffering from P.T.S.D. (Post Traumatic Scally Disorder). "What's eatin' you, Pop?" he asked, barely concerned.

Mr. Scally just looked over and glared at nature's mistake as his son grabbed a carton of orange juice from the refrigerator.

"And I'm not just sayin' that cause we're in the kitchen," the blonde Tasmanian devil added just before taking a swig of vitamin C straight from the container.

WRESTLING WITH JOEYLICIOUS

That got his father to snap out of his funk. "Get a glass, will you?!"

"It's all goin' down to the same place," Scally quipped.

"I didn't even know you could drink juice without your body going into shock." All you readers out there were probably thinking the same thing. This was the first and last non-alcoholic beverage for Scally in the entire book. He even spiked his one glass of water.

"I drink screwdrivers all the time." Hopefully, that explained it.

Mr. Scally could only shake his head in numbed disappointment as his son put the juice back, and plopped down at the table.

"How come mom never comes down? I haven't seen her since I've been back." Washi and Sayo's visit was fast approaching, so he needed to be certain that his old lady wouldn't suddenly reemerge.

"She's mourning the death of her son," his father said with a straight face.

This made little sense to Scally, but he decided to play along. "What son? You mean I had a long lost brother all this time?!"

"You! She's mourning you," Mr. Scally suddenly shouted, a whisker from a complete psychotic break. "She has been since you started high school."

Not the least bit fazed, the blonde troublemaker scoffed. "I finished high school in a year and a half!"

"High school finished with you! You barely passed your GED." Scally actually bribed the substitute teacher administering the GED exam with a case of imported beer in order to pass.

"I passed, didn't I?" Finished with the hellish trip down memory lane, he knew it was time to deal with the business at hand. "Listen, pop: you need to get out more. Why don't you go catch a flick? My treat." With that he placed a crisp $20 bill on the table. "It's not like mom is comin' down to make lunch anytime soon."

His father looked at the money suspiciously. Was it counterfeit? Would Scally yank back the bill just as he reached for it? Would it turn into dust later in his pocket just as he was stepping up to the ticket window? He quickly shook off each negative thought, and rubbed his chin as he considered the offer.

Scally knew that he had made a dent, but a dent wouldn't get his father out of the house. "The new Jason Statham one just opened. You're a fan! You have the entire Transporter Trilogy on Bluray!"

"He is good," Mr. Scally concurred, his mind and hand drawing closer to the $20.

"I think you should go right now." Scally stuffed the tantalizing bill into his father's shirt pocket, and escorted/pulled him toward the living room door.

This was definitely out of character, but the older Scally welcomed the sudden change in his son. He was clearly ready to give in. "You think?"

Scally smiled deviously. "I insist."

* * * * *

Back on the road, now only 100 miles from Hulkster heaven, Joey's stamina was holding up. The hair-raising nap he took somewhere in the Carolinas really did pay dividends. He glanced at the gas gauge, and smiled. With more than a half tank left, he was just going to make it. Probably. His mind started to drift. Beach shop, Hogan, beach shop, Hogan. He could practically taste victory. Imaginary Hogan, still sitting shotgun, seemed to be having the same happy thoughts.

It took the ringing of a cell to bring Joey and the Hulkster back to the present. Joey's mood even dampened when he read the caller ID. Nothing against Father Randazzo, of course, but it was "Sermon on the Mount" Sunday and he and the Civic were far, far away. Deciding to take his medicine, the Italian sinner answered the priest's call. "Hi, Father. Sorry I missed your big day."

Fr. Randazzo watched his parishioners leave as he stood in the back of Saint Thomas Aquinas church. His flock was waving their cheerful goodbyes, but the good priest was finding it difficult to reciprocate the notions. Even in his full Jesus costume, including a white robe, long brown hair, a beard, and blue contacts, Fr. Randazzo couldn't shake the disappointment regarding his one absent sheep. "On 'Sermon on the Mount' week?" he hissed, immediately letting Joey have it. "You promised me you'd start coming to mass!" He managed to fake a convincing smile as a male church member patted him on the back while passing. "Good to see you, Jerry."

"I'm driving to Tampa," Joey explained. "I thought my mom would've told you."

"You're talking to me while driving?" the priest shouted, suddenly less careful with his volume. "Put me on speaker!"

"Well, I'm sort of with someone-"

"Who? Scally?" Fr. Randazzo tore off his Jesus wig.

Again, Joey didn't want to explain. Seeing that his headset was in reach, he did his best to ignore the question as he leaned over the console. "Actually... Let me get my grab my headset-"

Hogan shifted his enormous rump as Joey pulled it out from

WRESTLING WITH JOEYLICIOUS

underneath him.

"Alright, Father," Joey continued, headset situated. "So how'd it go?"

Fr. Randazzo frowned. "Don't worry about how it went. Just show some support next time. I've been to your performances."

"I know. And I appreciate that." Joey wasn't placating the priest; he truly did.

"I have to go. These contacts are starting to dry out my eyes. But I'll see you next Sunday, right?" Fr. Randazzo figured he'd close with a mild threat for dramatic effect.

"Absolutely," Joey promised before hanging up.

Hogan gave a thoughtful look to the time just above the car stereo. "Lisch, I'd step on the gas if I were you."

"It's a Honda Civic. I take her anymore above 70, she might come apart on the road." Joey wasn't kidding. Even at its current speed, the car sounded like a tin can traveling over an erupting volcano.

"I probably arrive at my beach shop any minute now," Hogan pressed, coyly urging his not so young "pradagi" on.

"Probably?! Don't you even know what you're currently doing now?!" This seemed to be another one of those paradoxes.

Hogan sighed. "How could I?! I'm with you!"

"Man, the 'rules' of my imaginary hero sightings really suck," Joey muttered.

"Alright, take it easy, brother. Focus on the road."

Joey simmered down. What damage could a few more miles per hour actually do? He gently increased his foot's pressure on the gas, and left it at that.

Satisfied, Hogan moved on to other matters: "So what are you gonna say to me at the signing?"

Joey thought for a moment. "I don't know. I've been in such

a rush to get there, and then dealing with you... I haven't even really had time to think."

The Hulkster was shocked by the casual admittance of ill-preparedness. "You've been thinking of this upcoming moment your entire life!"

"I know, I know, it's just-"

"Please don't tell me you're gonna bring up the Sheik match? Or the Giant at Wrestlemania III?" Hogan was practically begging here.

The derision in his mentor's voice surprised Joey. "Why not?! Those are two of your biggest triumphs!"

"Every fan brings that up!" The Hulkster gestured wildly as if to encourage Joey to dig deeper. "You need to stand out if you wanna grab my attention, and pull me into the world of Joeylicious!"

Feeling that he understood where his number one hero was coming from, Joey racked his brain. "What if I mentioned the Ultimate Warrior match?" he said, finally coming up with a doozy.

Hogan was flabbergasted. And a little insulted. "When he pinned me for the belt at Wrestlemania VI?!"

Joey nodded, clearly proud of himself. "I would definitely stand out. How many fans of yours bring up defeats?"

"Standing out is one thing. But standing out in order to catch a beating is something else." Hogan's warning was immediate. As if Joey's beating could come sooner rather than later. Like in a moving Civic.

"Hulkster, that was an honorable defeat! And look at all the successes you've had since then," Joey persisted, wanting to win over the invisible legend with his point.

"Yeah, and look at me now - sitting here with you," Hogan replied dripping with sarcasm. Too easy, really.

WRESTLING WITH JOEYLICIOUS

"No, you're sitting at your beach shop in Tampa surrounded by hundreds of adoring fans," Joey retorted, doubling down.

At that, Hogan couldn't help but smile. It was progress at least. "Alright, brother. You win," he said, finally conceding the point.

Chapter 30

Samurai Dwayne

Scally paced the living room nervously. His expected guests were unexpectedly late. He looked at the time in an effort to stop it, but that just increased his anxiety. He wouldn't get another chance like this for a while. The next Jason Statham movie wouldn't be out for at least a year, and his mother could be roaming the house freely again by then. Gritting his teeth, he began to think that this was all in his head. Washi and Sayo didn't actually tell him they were coming over; he just imagined they did - like Joey imagined his wrestlers. Maybe his best friend and only client's condition was contagious!

But just when the "rapid firing sex machine" was about to give up all hope, a knock at the front door startled him out of his stupor. Rushing over, he yanked the door open and found Washi and Sayo standing on his parents' porch steps. He was relieved, excited and annoyed all at the same time. "You were supposed to be here over an hour an ago! What happened?!"

"We couldn't shake our ex," Sayo explained apologetically.

Scally looked between them, around them, and behind them, half expecting a charging sword to be coming at him. "Psycho-samurai?!"

Washi sighed. "Relax. We're here now, aren't we?"

Jumping out of the way, he ushered them into the house. "Come in, come in! My old man'll be back from the movies soon." Statham flicks didn't usually run past a 100 minutes. So even with the trailers, the sand in the hour glass was dwindling fast.

The two women stopped to take in the decor of the place. This was definitely a step up in property value compared to the arena of their first aborted encounter. Sayo was particularly impressed. "Nice house! Are we going upstairs?"

Scally placed a hand on her back, and steered her in the right direction. "Not a chance. But there's a couch in the basement."

"Makes no difference to me where we do it," Washi said, chiming in with her usual whatever-ness.

"Then it's settled!" He was already starting to undress.

They made little noise as they hurried down the basement stairs.

* * * * *

Joey was dripping wet in sweat. He was either incredibly pumped as he neared his destination, or the Florida heat was starting to get to him. The air condition on the Civic crapped out five years ago, and his mother never bothered to get it fixed. Regardless, he would soon be face to face with his hero. For real this time. He began to imagine how things would play out. Would beach shop Hogan be just as interested in helping him with his "budding" wrestling career as the Hogan sitting in the passenger seat was? It was easily the most exciting moment of his life.

Joey's imagination began to go into overdrive when flashing lights caught his attention. His eyes darted to the rearview mirror, and the reflection was not a happy one. "Would you believe this?!"

Hogan let out a heavy sigh. "Ah, that's too bad! He got you on radar."

WRESTLING WITH JOEYLICIOUS

"Damn it, Hulkster! Pay attention to these things! I'm driving!" He was too beside himself to realize that his imaginary being had its limits.

Hogan saw no need to defend himself to his creator. "Just pull over. You can't outrun the cops in a Civic," he responded calmly.

After slamming on the steering wheel, Joey accepted his misfortune. It was simply a price to pay. Meeting his idol was more than worth a speeding ticket.

The police car pulled up behind him.

Joey looked over at the legend sitting next to him. Maybe there was still a way out of this. "So you'll do the talking? Use your celebrity on him?"

"Brother, I'm not really here. How many times do we have to go over this?" Hogan was about ready to exit the car, and walk the rest of the way to the beach shop.

"Ugh! I keep forgetting!" This was followed by another slam on the steering wheel by the frustrated Italian.

A knock on the window forced Joey to get a hold of himself. He rolled down the glass partition and smiled. "Yes, hi officer. License and registration?"

The no nonsense cop nodded.

"Hulkster, can you reach into the glove-" For a second, Joey forgot again.

Hogan's expressionless face was all he needed to hear.

"Yeah, yeah, I know." Joey laughed awkwardly as he looked back at the cop in an effort to play that off. Then he leaned over, and opened the glove compartment all by his lonesome.

* * * * *

Mr. Scally returned from the movies feeling much better

about things. Once again, Jason Statham had helped the sun shine through the thick clouds of a stormy day. "Honey, I'm home," he called up to his wife. There was no immediate answer, so he upped his sales pitch: "Are you sure you don't wanna come down? Our dead son isn't around." Again no response, but he shrugged it off. Nothing was going to ruin this day. His son had even been respectful. That alone was something to celebrate.

He strolled over to the living room stereo, and threw on some smooth jazz. The older Scally always wanted to play like Kenny G, but didn't have the lips, ears or musical aptitude to even scratch the surface. To put it kindly, he was talentless. But as he sat down on the couch and relaxed, he was fine with that. Nothing was going to ruin this day.

A sudden rap at the front door immediately gave him second thoughts. Who would bother him on a Sunday afternoon? He definitely wasn't expecting anyone, so it had to be his son who forgot his key or something. Oh, well. So much for the relaxation. His son did treat him to Statham, so he had no choice but to let him in. But when he opened the door, he was both perplexed and frightened at what he saw. Standing on the porch wasn't a scrawny, five and a half foot tall, blonde Caucasian; it was a muscular, six and a half foot tall, African-American with a Samurai sword sheathed in a scabbard. Meet Samurai Dwayne.

Survival instincts kicking in, Mr. Scally wisely backed away from the door as the intimidating warrior entered on his own accord.

"Where are they?" The mysterious visitor's voice was just as scary as his physique.

Although a suspicion should have been forming in Mr. Scally's mind, he was too terrified to even imagine who or what Samurai Dwayne was referring to. "Who?! Where is who?!"

The stranger unsheathed his sword. "I'm not gonna ask again."

Mr. Scally panicked. "It's 2020! We're in Brooklyn! Why do you have a sword?!"

Samurai Dwayne's response was both simple and direct: he sliced the coffee table in half with his sword.

That single act was all the confirmation the older Scally needed. He calmed suddenly knowing he was off the hook. "Oh. You must be looking for my son."

"Is that the blonde midget I recently spotted my girls with?" the crazed swordsman asked, demanding more information.

"The one and only," Mr. Scally replied, neither demanding or even needing more information.

The guilty party peeked out from behind a quivering basement door, and was immediately spotted by the last person he wanted to be spotted by.

Samurai Dwayne pointed his sword. "You!" Of course, he didn't wait for a response as he charged the basement causing Scally to squeak and run back down the stairs.

Mr. Scally immediately heard the sounds of two unknown women echoing his son's cries during the unseen but quite imaginable raucous. He momentarily considered running upstairs to rescue his wife, but then thought better of it and just darted out of the house. Jason Statham he was not.

Seconds later, Scally, still in his tighty whities, scurried from the basement like a flesh colored rat with a bloodthirsty Samurai Dwayne in hot pursuit. The blonde weasel dove for cover behind the couch just as the angry stalker about cut him in half, destroying the leather piece of furniture instead.

A frantic Washi and Sayo emerged right behind the mayhem.

WRESTLING WITH JOEYLICIOUS

They were also still in their underwear, so round two between them and Scally obviously didn't get any further than round one. Still, they pleaded for their little man's life.

Samurai Dwayne would hear none of it. He continued to attack Scally and the room with equal gusto.

The scrawny blonde target miraculously ducked and weaved the razor sharp sword, but he had nowhere to hide. "I can see you're very talented," he shouted, trying his gift of gab on the vengeful ex. "Maybe we can do business together!"

Scally dodged another blow, but felt the wind from the blade as he lost a lock of hair. "Chocolate Milk Shake is a client of mine," he pleaded desperately. "You may know him!"

Samurai Dwayne would not be bargained with. He was not interested in the suspect manager's contract unless it was signed in the suspect manager's blood. All of it.

Realizing his diplomatic efforts were futile, Scally threw caution to the wind and sprinted for the door. He barely made it out alive, and the unrelenting swordsman stayed right on his coattails. Someone's cardio was about to be fully tested.

Washi and Sayo chased after their past, and future lovers (big maybe) with their continued screams attracting most of the neighborhood and the next neighborhood over.

Smooth jazz once again claimed the living room as the sounds of chaos faded down the streets of Brooklyn, New York.

Chapter 31

Imposter?!

Arriving in Tampa, Joey screeched to a halt as he double-parked the Honda Civic right in front of Hulk Hogan's beach shop. Understandably, the area was bustling with activity much like Joey was. He jumped out of the car, tucked his speeding ticket under one of the wipers to confuse any snooping cops, and ran to his hero's autograph signing. He would have made it straight inside if it wasn't for the dinosaur-sized security guard who gave him the stop sign.

"Nice outfit," the security guard snickered without snickering. Joey, of course, was still dressed as Joeylicious. He even had the stink of Tiny still on him, but the guard had his own hygiene issues to deal with.

"Thanks! I'm here to see the Hulkster! I'm his biggest fan!" The Italian Brooklynite was already hyperventilating.

The security guard scoffed. "Yeah, so are they." His thumb pointed to the ridiculous long line of fans that started at the shop and ended at infinity.

"You gotta be kidding me," Joey protested.

"I'm not, and they aren't either." Again with the thumb. This time it was used to point the so-called super fan to the back of the line.

Joey nodded, took a step toward infinity but stopped. He fought in too many crappy, elementary school gyms, and drove way too far in an equally crappy car to wait any longer. "There has to be some kind of arrangement we can work out."

"What'd you have in mind?" Obviously, the guard was open to negotiations. He needed to splurge on deodorant just as badly as Joey.

Joey thought of a reasonable price... "I'm challenging Paddy Shamrock for the belt next weekend. Brooklyn's Really Awesome Wrestling League-"

"BRAWL?" the security guard cut in with immediate recognition.

Joey couldn't believe his luck. "You heard of us?!"

Again the big man scoffed. "No. I took the first letter of each word you just said and spelled it out."

"How does a pair of ringside seats sound?" Whoever said Joey was easily deterred, didn't know the meaning of the words "easily" or "deterred." Or, they were legally insane.

"There are 11 Brooklyns in the US. None of them are in Florida." This was the guard's clever way of pointing to the back of the line again.

"What kind of silly talk is that?" Mr. Brooklyn shot back. "There's only one Brooklyn I know of. And that's the real one!"

"Look it up. It's a fact." It actually is.

"I left my smart phone in the car," Joey retorted. But he still felt negotiations were heading in the right direction. Somehow. "Do we have a deal?"

"Uh... no." The security guard finally put his negative stamp on the proceedings.

Joey's shoulders slouched in defeat. What else did he have to offer? He couldn't exactly wash dishes in this place. Maybe he could sand down a few surf boards. But before he threw that piece of summer gold on the table, Hulk Hogan's long time wrestling manager, "The Mouth of the South" Jimmy Hart, suddenly appeared. Sporting his customary shades, mustache, mullet and megaphone, he looked like he was on his way to or from a 1980s title match.

Wasting not a second, Jimmy dove head first into the negotiations: "C'mon, baby! Guys like us don't wait in line."

Instantly recognizing that voice, Joey turned with excitement. "Jimmy Hart! I knew you'd be here! You and the Hulkster have been buddies forever! It's an honor!" He grabbed the legendary manager's hand, and shook it vigorously for about a minute and a half.

Jimmy didn't seem to mind. In fact, he appreciated the Italian Dream's overenthusiastic enthusiasm. "Honor's all mine, Liscious! I've been following the indie scene for a while now, and I know all about you!"

"What? You've heard of me? I don't believe it!" Joey could have left right then and there, and his trip would've already been a success. But he wouldn't do that, would he?

"Yeah, baby! I'm always looking out for middle-aged talent like yourself to take under my wing and manage." Scally was suddenly on thin ice.

"'The Mouth of the South' wants to be my manager?! This is the greatest day of my life!" Scally then drowned in very cold water.

"It's about to get better!" The Mouth leaned in. "But first, do you have any cash on you? I only roll debit," he said with a whisper.

This was lost on Joey at first. "Uh..."

Jimmy pointed to the security guard as a reminder. "So we can grease this Neanderthal properly."

Joey started to nod. "Oh. Yeah. Uh..." He reached into his singlet and pulled out a soiled bill. "This is my last 50. I was saving for gas back home, but-"

The Mouth wasn't interested in hedging explanations, so he

~ 212 ~

just snatched Joey's nest egg from him. "Perfect!" He handed the money to the guard. "C'mon, baby! The Hulk is about to come out! I'll introduce you."

Joey could barely breath as he followed Jimmy into the beach shop. "I think I'm gonna pass out."

The place was packed to the gills with Hulk Hogan fans.

Joey collected himself. "Mouth, look at this crowd! Do you think it could be like this for me one day?"

"When I'm in your corner, every day is like this, baby!" What Jimmy lacked in modern fashion sense, he made up for in confidence.

Joey's euphoria was interrupted when a random surfer dude smacked into him with his surfboard.

"Hey, watch it with that thing," Joey protested, rubbing his shoulder.

The surfer turned unaware of his transgression. Whatever he was going to say quickly faded from memory as he took in Joey's outfit. "Are you supposed to be a superhero or something?"

"Or something," the proud indie wrestler responded curtly. "The name's Joeylicious."

"Sounds like you're on the wrong end of a glory hole." In fairness to Joey, he came up with the name well before such pleasure constructs were invented.

But he was insulted just the same. "Why are you even here?! It looks like you're just on your way to the beach!"

"I am on my way to the beach," the surfer barked back. "This is a beach shop. Or perhaps you missed the sign."

Joey latched onto that remark. "This is the Hulkster's beach shop," he shouted, pointing out the missing detail. "And don't you ever forget it!"

The surfer scoffed. "Fair enough. But you wanna know what

I will forget?"

"What?" Joey wasn't really curious, but he was boxed into having to ask.

"You." And with that the surfer turned, and continued toward his usual habitat.

"Kids these days," Jimmy muttered. "No respect."

"Tell me about it, Mouth." Joey appreciated a manager who was fully on his side for once. He knew Scally's heart was in the right place, but his mouth and brain were somewhere south of wrong.

The unpleasant interaction was quickly forgotten as the crowd began to perk up and clamor. Something was afoot, and Joey turned to see what it was.

A familiar looking figure with his arms raised in triumph stepped out from behind a beaded curtain near the signing table. The place went ballistic, but Joey could sense something was amiss. The cherished figure, although resembling Hulk Hogan, was a little too short, a bit too old, and clearly too out of shape to be the real deal.

Beside him, Jimmy immediately mouthed Joey's inner suspicions: "What the hell is this? That's not the Hulk, baby!"

Joey clenched his fists. "I can't believe it! That's some stupid impersonator! Why are these morons cheering?" He was already ready to punch someone.

"Let's give him a piece of our mind," the Mouth said, urging his new client on. "Whattaya say, Liscious?"

"Absolutely, Mouth! I'm gonna lay into this fool!" Again, this was the type of manager Joey always wanted and needed.

With that, they pushed their way forward through the crowd until they were close enough to the signing table. "Booo! Go home, you wannabe," Joey shouted over everyone.

This got immediate attention from the fans. Shocked heads

WRESTLING WITH JOEYLICIOUS

turned to the oncoming agitator, and some even cleared a path. Joey was dressed like a wrestler, so perhaps he was just part of the show.

Joey took notice of the crowd noticing him. "What? You wanna piece of Joeylicious?! The man of the hour, the tower of power, too sweet to be sour, the Italian Dream-"

"That's a lotta nicknames, Lisch," Jimmy mumbled beside him.

Like a laser, Joey pointed at the fake wrestling legend now sitting at the table. "Get that imposter outta here!"

Of course, this got the Mouth's full support. "You tell 'em!"

When they reached the imposter, Joey glared down at him.

The Hogan look-alike may have been concerned at the crazed wrestling fan before him, but he played it off with good humor: "Hey, brother! Nice boas! What can I sign for you?"

Joey was insulted by the offer. "Mouth, look at this fraud. His mustache isn't even real!" Without waiting for a response or an invitation, he reached out and tugged on the so-called facial hair. It was real. And the stunt turned the imposter's amused expression into one of surprised annoyance.

"Okay, so anyone can grow a mustache," Jimmy said, quick to dismiss the blonde whiskers.

Recovering from the shock of the face yanking, the Hogan look-alike growled. "What the hell, brother?! What's your problem?"

Joey wasn't the least bit deterred. "You're not a wrestler! You're just some fake! I'm a real wrestler! Mouth, watch this!" He slapped the "imposter" hard across the face.

The crowd gasped at the blatant disrespect for their hero. "Oh, snap," several even shouted.

But Joey was proud of his outrageous act. He was speaking for all wrestling fans from around the world. Or at least the ones between Brooklyn and Tampa. He gave his would-be idol one final intimidating stare down. "That's what you get for making me drive all the way from Brooklyn for a lame impersonator," he spat. Turning on his heels, he then motioned for Jimmy to join him. "C'mon, Mouth. Let's get outta here!"

"You said it, baby." Like a proud papa, the Mouth of the South put his arm around his new client as they headed toward the exit.

The Hogan look-alike stood up. Only he didn't look much like an imposter anymore. This new and improved Hogan was suddenly taller, muscular and angrier. "Hold on a second there, brother."

Joey froze halfway to the door. That voice sounded a little more familiar than before. And a lot more frightening.

Relishing the upcoming event, the crowd parted like the red sea for their blonde giant without as much as a murmur.

With the sound of menacing footsteps heading his way, Joey looked to his new manager for an explanation. "Mouth, what's up?"

But Jimmy wasn't there. Knowing all to well what that meant by now, Joey gulped and nervously turned to face the music. And he knew the music would be loud. Standing directly over him was the legend he had idolized his entire wrestling life. This, of course, was the real Hulk Hogan after all.

"Hulk?" Joey asked as much as pleaded.

It was far too little, too late as the Hulkster let his fist respond. Joey took the punch square in the face, and immediately felt time slow to a crawl as he keeled over backwards. He lost consciousness before he hit the floor.

The crowd erupted in cheers and applause. This was the kind of entertainment they had not expected, but certainly

WRESTLING WITH JOEYLICIOUS

appreciated.

Real Hogan looked down at the wannabe wrestler with disappointment. "What a jerk. And a shame, too. I really liked his look. Could've helped him become a superstar. Oh, well..." With that he headed back to the signing table, leaving Joey passed out on the floor.

"Next," the Hulkster called out to another round of cheers.

The next person in line stepped over the motionless Joey, and posed for a picture with their blonde hero.

Joey slept through the rest of the event like a bloodless corpse left on the battlefield. At least he would be well rested for his long, painful ride home. If he could only find money for gas...

Epilogue

At the Pro Wrestling headquarters in Philadelphia, Pennsylvania, Executive Vice President, Erica Martin, World Wrestling Champion, Chris Jericho, and his manager, Steven Brown were in the middle of a heated discussion in Erica's office.

Brown currently had the floor. "Whattaya mean, he has a conflict?! This is for the Heavyweight Title! Isn't Farley under contract with us?"

Erica sighed as if they had already been over this a dozen times. "Of course, he's under contract with us, but it stipulates that he won't wrestle on the Sabbath. It's in fine print."

Jericho's frustrated manager threw up his hands and flopped back in his chair. "Then why the hell did we schedule our biggest match of the year on a Saturday?"

"Like I said, the fine print," the executive reiterated. Again. "We didn't even know he was Jewish."

"That's because he's not Jewish, for Chrissake!" Brown was beside himself.

"Then why won't he wrestle on a Saturday?" Erica countered.

"Because he's a nut," Brown countered her counter. He figured that was at least obvious.

Finally, a significantly calmer Jericho offered his two cents: "Steve-O, chill out, man. I totally understand. He's a religious butterfly extending his wings out to God. It reminds me of the time I went on a spiritual retreat with Zsa Zsa Gabore back in

WRESTLING WITH JOEYLICIOUS

the early 90s. We went to Bucharest, and locked ourselves in a 200 degree tent for six hours."

Whatever that was, it was all said with a quasi British accent that threw Erica for a loop. She looked to the Champ's manager with confusion.

Jericho continued to reminisce as if he was a Duke on the autistic spectrum. "Zsa Zsa got quite frisky that night if I recall."

"Why is Chris talking like this?" the executive whispered to Brown. "He sounds like Mr. Howell from Gilligan's Island."

The manager waved away her concerns. "It's his new shtick. I think he sounds more like that L. Ron Hubbard guy." He actually sounded like a cross between the Count of Monte Cristo and Orville Redenbacher, but why get technical? "By the way, address him as 'Christoff' from now on. The Champ feels it's more consistent with the accent."

"What are you two darlings humming about?" the newly christened Christoff interrupted, chiding them playfully. "There are no secrets here."

His manager forced a smile. "It's nothing, Champ."

With bigger fish to fry, Erica dropped her query into Jericho's new peculiarity. "Farley just gave notice that his clause has been exercised. My hands are tied."

But the Champ continued to butt in from the other side of the pond: "Speaking of exercise, I just returned from my Pilates class with Joyce Dewitt and Loloa Falana, and you're both interfering with my 70's infused Zen."

Brown did his best to politely ignore his transitioning client as he stayed on Erica. "How did you not see this coming? We've been working on this story line for six months. Jericho turns-" He realized his mistake immediately. "I mean, Christoff turns babyface."

~ 219 ~

"Stevie honey, I told you what my therapist said," Jericho chimed in yet again.

"I know, Champ," Brown reassured him, "No more 'Mr. Dad Guy.' Hence, the babyface turn."

"At least til I work out some childhood issues." Did his therapist also inspire the aristocratic accent?

Brown refocused with Erica. "So what else? Have you talked to the writers? We're a little short on time here. It would be nice to actually promote this match."

Erica wasn't entirely discouraged. "There are some ideas we're spitballing," she said.

"Shoot." Brown was all ears.

She began to fill the manager in: "If Chris suddenly had something to overcome-"

"Christoff," Brown corrected.

"If Christoff suddenly had something to overcome before the match. Like an illness, or a personal tragedy-"

Jericho immediately had his reservations. "Nothing negative. I'm trying to be one with the universe."

"Scratch that," his manager concurred.

Erica twisted her mouth in contemplation. "What about a long, lost relative coming back into the fold?"

Jericho gave her an enigmatic look. "I actually have a long, lost relative."

Thinking she may have hit the mark, Erica demanded a quick elaboration. "And?"

The Champ's response was entirely anticlimactic: "I'd rather he didn't come back into the fold."

Feeling a bit of a letdown himself, Brown turned back to Erica. "You were saying?"

But Jericho wasn't finished. He had another non-sequitur floating around in his head. "Do you know what was on TCM last night?"

Erica looked to Brown over this new, bizarre interjection.

The Champ ignored the executive's quizzical outreach. "The most spiritually uplifting movie of all time," he continued.

"Schindler's List?" Brown offered.

"Gandhi?" Erica guessed.

Jericho sighed at their quick-triggered responses. They both witnessed athletic glory of the highest order on the sidelines of many packed arenas, so the answer should have been an obvious one. "Come now, my lovelies. This was about a tremendous human being. His story is like a flower floating through the air searching for its pedestal."

Not a clue on where his client was going with this, Brown pulled the only film Stephen King ever directed out of his managerial hat. "Maximum Overdrive?"

Erica tried to be more consistent with the Champ's clue, while staying on Brown's train of thought. "The Mighty Ducks?" Well, both films did star Martin Sheen's oldest son.

Jericho was so frustrated with them, he momentarily lost his British accent. "How does anything I just said ring the bell of an Emilio Estevez double feature? Rocky!"

For some reason his manager wanted immediate clarification. "Which one?"

But Jericho suddenly segued again as his accent returned: "Although, I did have brunch with Emilio on a yacht in Madrid back in '06. Such a lovely man-"

Brown reeled his eccentric wrestler back to the Philadelphia headquarters. "Champ, which Rocky did you see?"

Jericho reemerged. "The one with Apollo Creed."

His manager pursed his lips. "He was in four of them."

"When they fought."

"They fought twice."

"Three times," Erica cut in, correcting the misinformed manager.

"Apollo was Rocky's manager in part three," Brown quickly pointed out.

"But they fought at the end."

Brown waved away her explanation. "As a favor to Apollo. That was nothing."

The executive rubbed her chin. "Didn't Apollo also fight in four?"

"Not against Rocky. That was the Russian." Brown really knew his Carl Weathers.

It finally sunk in with Erica. "Right, when he got killed-"

Jericho had enough of their unfocused exchange. "Ladies, and gentlemen, please!"

They quit their banter.

Then Jericho finally put the matter to bed. "It was the first one..." (or did he?) "when Apollo gave an unknown a shot at the title."

Erica and Brown took a moment to absorb that. The Champ just wittingly or unwittingly solved their problem. They would give an unknown, non-Sabbath observing wrestler the chance of a lifetime.

Erica tapped her mouth and smiled. "I love it."

To Be Continued…

Wrestling with Joeylicious

NOW AVAILABLE ON

amazon prime video

STARRING THE LEGENDS OF WRESTLING

Joey   **Scally**

Where it all began. Joey & Scally's 6th grade class picture.
If only Miss Whalen knew what she was in for...

1984: Joey & Scally pumped up in the schoolyard. Later that night they will witness Hulk Hogan win the WWF title!

A Young 10yr old Rob Scally "I've never even seen an M-80! Why blame me for the girls bathroom toilet?"

Wrestling with Joeylicious

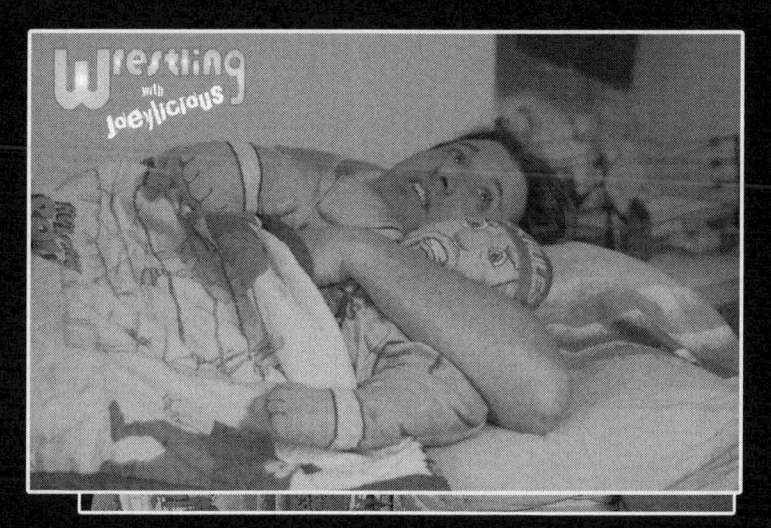

The Italian Dream getting a little too cozy with his hero.

Buy one ticket to this Saturday's event, get two free!

B.R.A.W.L!
Brooklyn's Really Awesome Wrestling League

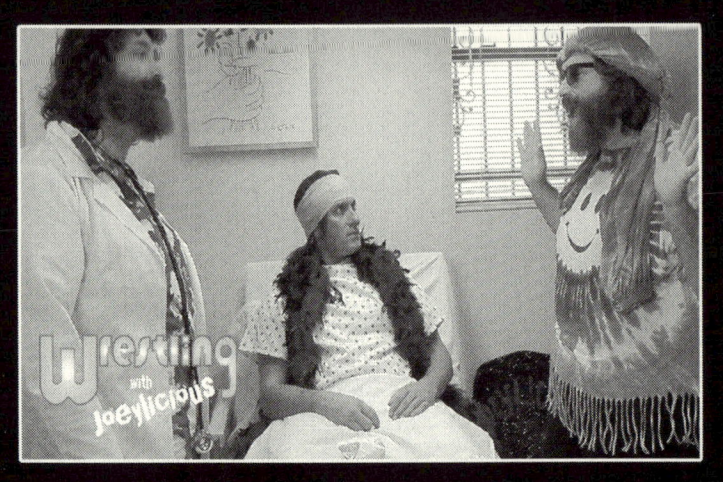

Is Joey seeing double? Or is the Micker a master illusionist?

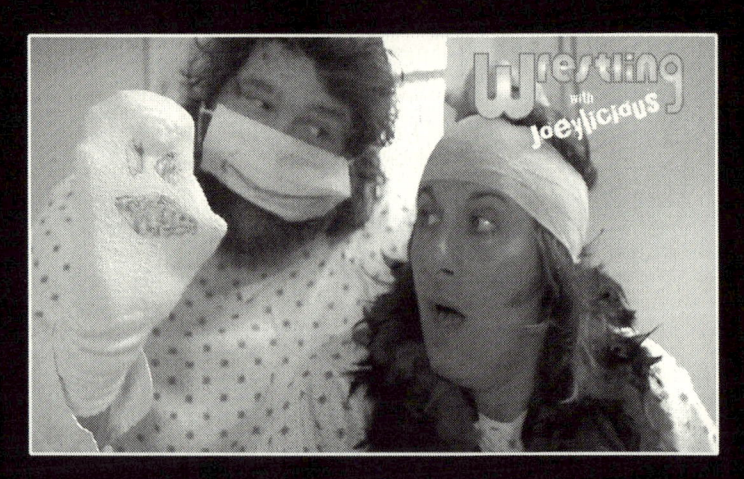

Joey ignoring a legend's advice at his own peril. Again.

I always wondered what The Hot Rod was wearing under there.

Joey & 'The Mouth of the South' on their way to deal with the Hulkster Imposter!

Wrestling with Joeylicious

Preview of a Future Title Match?...

About the Authors

On January 21, 1974, a bolt of lightning flashed across the sky, the seas roared, the ground shook, and Joseph Michael Cassata and Christopher Lynn (no middle name) were each born, brothers from another mother in Brooklyn, New York. Growing up a mere four blocks from each other in the neighborhood still known today as Marine Park, they both attended St. Thomas Aquinas Elementary School where they crossed paths for the first time. It was here, in the lunchroom of S.T.A., that the great swindle of 1985 took place. Joey, an avid Kiss fan, and Chris, an avid baseball fan, sat down and completed, what was believed to be, a fair trade at the time. Joey got four Mego Kiss dolls, and Chris got some baseball paraphernalia including Mike Pagliarula's NY Yankees rookie card. Pagliarula's career started out promising but fizzled out rather quickly. None of the members of Kiss, on the other hand, ever lost their shine. 4'3 Robert Scally, another S.T.A. alumni, mediated the lopsided deal, but was secretly scheming for Joey at the time. He got half an Ace Frehley doll for his troubles. Because of this transactional travesty, it was years before Joey and Chris ever spoke again.

Finally, after a night of recreational drinking in separate bars on Flatbush Avenue, they bumped into each other at Lenny & John's Pizzeria at 2AM on a random Saturday. The pizza always tasted best then. After apologizing for his childhood trickery, Joey told Chris about his lifelong dream to become a professional wrestler. (By the way, Chris accepted Joey's apology after a mutual toast of steaming hot, meat rice balls.) Once Chris reminded Joey that he was only 5'10, 180lbs and already over 40, the two long lost pals decided to write a book about wrestling instead. And the rest is history. Or present - depending on whether you're reading this "About the Authors" section before or after you read the book.

Made in the USA
Coppell, TX
31 March 2022